C000173700

TIME STOOD STILL IN A MUDDY HOLE

TIME STOOD STILL IN A MUDDY HOLE

CAPTAIN JOHN HANNAFORD

One of the last Bomb Disposal Officers of WWII

PAT STRICKSON

First published 2018

Copyright © Patricia Strickson 2018

The right of Patricia Strickson to be identified as the author of this work has been asserted in accordance with the Copyright, Designs & Patents Act 1988.

All rights reserved. No part of this book may be reproduced, stored in a retrieval system, or transmitted in any form or by any means, electronic, electrostatic, magnetic tape, mechanical, photocopying, recording or otherwise, without the written permission of the copyright holder.

Published under licence by Brown Dog Books and
The Self-Publishing Partnership, 7 Green Park Station, Bath BA1 1JB

www.selfpublishingpartnership.co.uk

ISBN printed book: 978-1-78545-286-4

ISBN e-book: 978-1-78545-294-9

Cover design by Kevin Rylands
Internal design by Andrew Easton

Printed and bound in the UK

Dedicated to my father,
Alexander Sinclair

1928-2017

TABLE OF CONTENTS

FOREWORD

I was delighted to have been asked to write this introduction to Pat Strickson's book on Captain John Hannaford, who was one of the last surviving Bomb Disposal officers of the Second World War.

When I commanded a Royal Engineer Bomb Disposal Squadron in the mid-1970s, we dealt with a tiny fraction of the number of bombs which John Hannaford defuzed during the Second World War. Our work with old German bombs was made far easier by having detailed instruction manuals; however, Bomb Disposal officers dealing with them during the Second World War often faced a dangerous unknown. Although our equipment was more modern, the procedures and techniques we used to keep us safe were the same ones which John and his colleagues had developed, frequently at great cost to their lives, some 30 years earlier. Similar methodical procedures are used by modern Bomb Disposal officers to deal with terrorist bombs today. We owe these brave men a great debt.

John Hannaford did not volunteer for Bomb Disposal duties but, when he was selected, performed that role courageously. Pat Strickson's book is a fitting tribute to him.

Roderick MacArthur
Lieutenant Colonel (Retired)
Chairman
Royal Engineer Bomb Disposal Officers Club

A percentage of the proceeds of this book will support the **Felix Fund**. The **Felix Fund** is a triservice charity set up to support serving and ex-serving Bomb Disposal experts and their families through therapeutic breaks, other welfare and rehabilitation facilities and hardship grants.

NOTE FROM JOHN HANNAFORD

'It is strange but true that the war input of Royal Engineer Bomb Disposal seemed to be wiped out of memory and war history the moment WWII ended. At meetings and parties the chat was always dominated by ex-RAF veterans about their exploits.

For the record I never held it against them. They did magnificently.

It was not until Afghanistan and its media coverage of the lethal effect of IEDs that the nation's memory went back to WWII and the devastating bombing of the UK that we ex-WWII Bomb Disposal began to be asked, "How on earth did you do it?"

That little niggle that lasted so many years was finally expunged and I feel that so many who lost their lives were at last remembered and received belated credit for what they had endured.'

ACKNOWLEDGEMENTS

I could not have written this amazing story without the help of some wonderful people.

Thank you to Emily Vane of Picture Crafts who, on that first day captured my imagination by her infectious enthusiasm for Captain John Hannaford's story.

A heartfelt thank-you to John's daughters, Jill Buch and Jackie Medley, for their continued support and for answering all my emails, texts and queries, and for sharing memories of both their mother and their father.

I am indebted to Steve Venus, John's friend, expert collector of WWII fuzes, bombs and memorabilia, who shared his enthusiasm and his collection. He has always been there to help me with the technicalities of a totally new subject.

I am immensely indebted to the Chairman of the Royal Engineers Bomb Disposal Officers Club, Lieutenant Colonel Roderick MacArthur of the Royal Engineers, retired Bomb Disposal Squadron Commander 1976-77. He generously shared his expertise, time and comprehensive Bomb Disposal knowledge from WWII to the present day, even giving my husband and I a presentation in our home along with his dear wife Hazel, and for meeting us in Malta when the coincidental occasion arose to support John's story further.

I am also extremely grateful to John Dowling, a much-admired local journalist. He generously gave me his first-hand knowledge of conversations with John Hannaford and shared his important last interview only months before, also for allowing me to access and use his photographs and report about the Catsfield story.

To the inspirational authors I've come into contact with through John's story: Andrea Samuelson, Susan Hudson and Kerin Freeman, thank you for your passion and for your craft.

To James Owen and M J Jappy, a special thank-you for their excellent books that helped me better understand the life of the WWII Bomb Disposal teams.

To Penny Brace for her kindness, local knowledge and wonderful Welsh hospitality.

Thank you to the *Tenby Observer* and the *Chepstow Beacon* for spreading the word, and to Steven John, a historian from South Wales, for helping me to find the forgotten men of 8 Section.

To the staff of the National Archives at Kew a huge vote of appreciation for their help and excellent resources. A special thank-you to their Education Manager, Rachel Hillman, whom I remember fondly as an enthusiastic and hard-working young teacher at Hellingly CP School in East Sussex and who gave me confidence to carry on researching this story.

Sincere wishes to Bexhill Museum, the Royal Engineers and their excellent site, the Imperial War Museum, Chapel Bay Fort and Museum, Saundersfoot Historical Society and the National Museum of Malta in Valletta for their background knowledge and expertise.

To Tracey Bartlett, a wonderful teacher and computer expert who helped me with the next steps in presentation for writing.

To all of my many friends, new and old, who have been supportive throughout this thoroughly engrossing story, I thank you from the bottom of my heart.

To my dear husband Harry, my amazing mother Helen and my wonderful daughters Jennifer and Caroline, my son-in-law Robert, Barnaby and Audrey, my grandchildren, always a welcome distraction and to all my family, my love and special thanks to each of you.

ABBREVIATIONS

AFJ Hannaford ARIBA - Avro Frederick John Hannaford, ARIBA, Associate of the Royal Institute of British Architects

Ack-Ack guns - Anti-Aircraft guns

AVRO K504 - **A**lliott **V**erdon **Ro**e, designer of K504 planes in WWI. Pilot Tom Hannaford flew in one.

BD - Bomb Disposal

CO - Commanding Officer

IED - Improvised Explosive Device

IF & DBD - Department where Scientists uncovered the secrets of Fuzes

IWM - Imperial War Museum

Lt Col - Lieutenant Colonel

MP - Military Police

RDX - A stable explosive, which needs a detonator to explode. It was commonly used in WWII.

RE - Royal Engineers

ROF - Royal Ordnance Factory

TNT - Trinitrotoluene, an explosive used in bomb-making

UXB - Unexploded bomb

WWII - World War Two

MEANINGS

Sapper A private soldier in the Royal Engineers. A soldier responsible for tasks such as building roads and bridges, digging for bombs, and laying and clearing mines.

FUZE / DEFUZED

In John Hannaford's notes and research books about bomb disposal I noticed the spelling used when describing dismantling a bomb and making it safe was **fuze**. I'd expected it spelt as **fuse** and made a mental note to check.

Chairman of the Royal Engineers Bomb Disposal Officers Club, Lieutenant Colonel Rod MacArthur and WWII collector of fuzes and friend of Captain Hannaford's, Steve Venus, both explained it clearly to me.

So if, like me, you questioned the spelling, please be reassured that it is spelt correctly in this instance when describing the delicate and dangerous dismantling of bombs.

John also chose to spell it that way in his notes, and therefore I have followed the expert's guidance.

The dictionary points out that a **fuze** is a device with explosive components designed to initiate a main charge.

A **fuse** is a cord or tube for the transmission of flames and explosion with gunpowder, or when a **fuse** is part of an electrical circuit.

John's 17 fuze. A slight imperfection allowed him to remove it, 'one nick away from destruction.'

Part of Steve Venus' collection

De La Warr Pavilion painted by AF J Hannaford

As a retired Headteacher I searched for a new and absorbing interest.

It was a remarkable afternoon when I found Captain John Hannaford's painting. My discovery that the artist was a war hero transported me back to a period in WWII when there was a real threat of invasion for our country, a fervour and urgency to life, and when young people had little choice about their futures. I learnt about the destructive and disruptive nature of unexploded bombs, or UXBs, that rained down on us. It was shocking to find out that increasingly those UXBs were booby-trapped to kill and maim soldiers like Captain Hannaford, whose wartime job it was to disarm and dispose of them.

CHAPTER I
UNSUNG HERO

It all started on a cold winter's day in February 2016. It seemed an unlikely day for such a stroke of luck, but that day I discovered AFJ Hannaford my life changed.

It was a miserable Saturday afternoon. The drizzle that shrouded the small seaside town of Bexhill in its drenching grey curtain had been on since morning. People were hurrying along to get their weekend shop done, to get out of the rain, and to get home. That was my idea, too, but I had to wait for my husband who was at the optician's.

The warm lights of the Cancer Research charity shop looked inviting. I had ten minutes to spare. It was definitely one of those days to be indoors, lost in a good book. So I made my way through the busy shop to find one, but before I reached the books, my eyes were drawn by the ceiling light shining on a watercolour of the De La Warr Pavilion, just above the bookcase. My eyes fixed on the iconic building that was at that moment surrounded in mist at the end of the road. Facing across the English Channel, it proudly overlooks the wide promenade with the sea stretching beyond. Eastbourne and Beachy Head are to the west, Hastings,

Rye and Dungeness to the east. The building, with its shell-like staircase, is designed with many windows reflecting that usually sparkling sea that was hidden from view that afternoon. The building's balcony resembles the decks of an elegant cruise ship, the result of a competition in the 1930s. It was commissioned by the 9th Earl De La Warr and designed by winning architects Erich Mendelsohn and Serge Chermayeff. It's a modernist work of art. I visit there often to see the exhibitions. It's at the heart of the town. My walks end there. We take visitors there and it's where I meet friends for coffee. Now it was filling my view and my thoughts with good memories which all rushed through my mind as I stared up at it.

It was obvious the watercolour artist admired the building too. It was painted in an oval with careful attention to detail. The windows reflected the soft sea light. The clean lines of its creamy walls contrasted with the deep purple shadows and were surrounded by swathes of manicured grass and a clear blue sky. It had been painted a few years before, as an extension for an education room and a new water feature were missing. The painting told a story. There were many families, sunseekers enjoying the fine summer's day. They were heading down to the beach laden with baskets and towels. It was a busy picture and a pleasure to see such a happy scene on a dreary afternoon. It warmed me right through.

Carefully I took it down. It was original and was signed by the artist, AFJ Hannaford. Why was it not framed? Why was it there at all and in an old, taped plastic bag? The watercolour paper was of good quality and weight. Other shoppers looked over my shoulder also admiring it. A few made comments trying to guess about the artist.

'It must be a man,' said one. 'It's so detailed and precise in composition.'

I already felt protective of the painting and quickly headed to the counter. There was no bag big enough for its A3 size so I tucked it carefully under my coat and headed off into the rain. I nipped into the optician's briefly, explaining to my bemused husband about the painting.

'It deserves to be framed, don't you think?' Without waiting for an answer, I said, 'I'll take it now.'

Luckily, he agreed.

As I entered the framers, Emily greeted me. She'd helped me on several previous occasions. I carefully produced the watercolour, saying how lucky I'd been to find it. I unwrapped the plastic to show her.

Immediately she said, 'I know that painting. I made copies for the old gentleman to give to his friends. My measurements are on the back.'

I turned it over and, sure enough, there they were, her pencilled numbers.

She continued, 'He was a war hero, you know.' She said it with such feeling. She'd liked him. 'He was quite a character,' she said, coming into the shop on several occasions, not always easy to please. They'd had many conversations. I envied her in that moment.

It was a lot to take in. I already knew I was pleased to own something painted by this man. My love of the watercolour now extended to the pleasure of owning a work by a wartime hero. How amazing!

Her eyes shone. Mine, too. 'Let me show you,' she said.

In the empty shop Emily turned the screen on the counter as she typed his name. Artist AFJ Hannaford appeared as Captain John Hannaford, Royal Engineers Bomb Disposal officer from WWII. We read on.

Within seconds a number of obituaries appeared from several national newspapers and the local *Bexhill-on-Sea Observer*. They said he was one of the last bomb disposal officers of WWII. John Hannaford died on Armistice Day, 11th November 2015, at the grand age of 98, five days after his wife Joyce. They had been together over 60 years. The family had celebrated their lives with a joint funeral. Both had experienced traumatic events in World War Two. Joyce had lost her first husband at the last great but disastrous battle at Arnhem in Belgium, a battle that I discovered later had many needless fatalities. She was eight months pregnant at the time. John served in the Royal Engineers in one of the first bomb disposal squads, in what has been described for me as one of the most dangerous jobs in the war, deactivating and removing unexploded bombs, or UXBs.

The obituaries reported he had survived several near misses and witnessed the deaths and horrific injuries of colleagues and friends. He was described as an unsung hero. He disagreed, saying those same colleagues and friends who gave their young lives for our country were the true heroes.

Captain Hannaford's last interview in Oct 2015

In his last interview in October 2015, a month before he died, local journalist John Dowling's title was 'Last Bomb Disposal Officer', and he took this photograph as Captain Hannaford shared his photograph album. He reported Captain Hannaford's story and passionate plea that they be remembered, as he felt they were forgotten in history. It was stirring stuff. When my husband appeared, he, too, read the articles and marvelled at the artist's story and the dangerous and daring jobs the bomb disposal teams tackled in WWII.

We discussed the painting at some length, now savouring its

important link with the past. With the frame chosen, we set off home. How the day had changed: from dull to illuminated, as if a light had been switched on and brought to life by the artist!

Finding John Hannaford was better than any book. I followed his story and picked up where we'd left off. But now it unfolded at home on my computer. Reading the obituaries again I began to piece together his life. Just like a good book, time was irrelevant. It was an engrossing few hours that first afternoon.

I shared the story of the painting with my family and friends. I discovered their stories and an amazing family link. My great-uncle had also served in bomb disposal in WWII and had survived the war. I hadn't been aware of his wartime work. Soon I had his photos and memorabilia, too, and importantly his training notebook. Could he have met Captain Hannaford? Their paths may have crossed. My mother said her uncle never spoke to her of his dangerous work, but she was very young, only eleven in 1945 as the war ended. He would have been ordered not to divulge the details of his job. I'd already learnt of the secrecy surrounding bomb disposal in the wartime press. The soldiers were told their work was top secret, and that came from Winston Churchill himself. Captain Hannaford said in his interviews that they were told not to talk of their important work for fear of giving the enemy vital information or damaging civilian morale following the devastating effect of the heavy bombing raids. I later was to find out his own family knew little of his job in the war until many decades later when he retired.

Avro Frederick John Hannaford: his name seemed like an adventure in itself. His life had been an extraordinary one filled with dangerous deeds, followed by a long and successful career. But in that last interview there was little mention of his post-war job, just how unhappy he was and so disappointed that the men of WWII Bomb Disposal had been forgotten. How could that be? I felt bewildered by that statement. As I learnt his story I was in awe of those brave bomb disposal soldiers, as were others I discussed it with. How had he wanted their work recorded and in what historical context? I had to find out. His family were mentioned. I felt I needed to contact them to find out more and ask their permission to continue.

In the next few days I felt like a detective, reflecting on what I'd already learnt and how I planned the next steps. Firstly I checked online. An address appeared in St Leonards, Hastings. Surprisingly I knew it, another coincidence, having visited the house opposite only a month or so before. It must have been his previous home. It was a large family house. I learnt he was Chief Architect for the South of England. It was secluded, positioned high on a hill looking over towards the sea and Pevensey Bay, the landing place for Duke William of Normandy on his route to the Battle of Hastings to fight King Harold and his men. King Harold was weary from another battle he and his men had won in the north. They'd marched hundreds of miles to fight William's strong Norman army.

John Hannaford liked living in '1066 country'. It was the place where our country's history changed dramatically. He himself had lived through and played a key role in the dramatic change in our recent history.

Mines had been laid along those same beaches to deter a German invasion, as they were laid all around the coast of Britain. Those mines were laid then removed by Royal Engineer Bomb Disposal units, and many were injured or killed doing that dangerous work. John Hannaford still mourned the deaths of his men in South Wales who died clearing mines from the beaches.

I continued my search for John Hannaford's home as I was told by Emily he had lived in a flat on the seafront in Bexhill. I looked up the local telephone directory and there was his name with the address. I felt the connection with him even more strongly now I had his telephone number. Why was I surprised? He'd lived there only three months before. But it was a good result. I wondered if his family were selling the property? That was probably the reason the painting had turned up in the charity shop.

I checked on the Internet again. I searched 'flats for sale', and sure enough, a local estate agent was advertising the property. I went through the photos of the rooms imagining where AFJ Hannaford the artist had painted. It still had his and his wife's furnishings. I felt as though I was trespassing. Then his words about his men came back to mind: I knew I had to keep going.

My research told of nearly 50,000 unexploded bombs excavated, defuzed and made safe by men of the Royal Engineer Bomb Disposal squads here in our country. I tried hard to imagine the scenes, the noises of air-raid sirens, planes screeching overhead, the whistling of a bomb, the silence, delayed destruction, the dust settling and the resulting horror. I remembered newsreels and recent commemorative news programmes that had much more meaning now. I wished I'd listened more closely. Whole teams blown up, he'd said! This was coming to life here and now in my own home. Finding out that John Hannaford felt so disappointed spurred me on. He'd said he saw men die. He questioned: why had he been so lucky?

I made my way to the estate agents, hesitating before I entered. I collected my thoughts. Once inside, my enthusiasm took over. Words tumbled out in my nervousness to explain about my discovery, about Captain Hannaford and his heroic work. The man greeting me had read the newspaper story and was also interested to know more. I knew it so well now: why had I not paid more attention and read the local paper I get delivered? But I was wrapped up in my own family matters. I asked if it was possible that they put me in touch with his family. The manager couldn't put me directly in contact but said he would let the family know. A couple of days later, I had the message I hoped for. John Hannaford's daughter would be pleased to hear from me.

I carefully wrote the letter, introducing myself and explaining about the painting and my wish to write about her father. Until that moment I hadn't dared admit to myself that that was actually what I wanted to do. Could I do him justice? I knew I'd try my very best.

I'd never written a book – a thesis was the nearest to it, for my MA. But that had been a necessary part of my studies as I continued my career as a teacher. That was work. This was already different. This story was important and needed to be told. I felt driven. People needed to know what John Hannaford felt so passionate about.

I'd written many reports as a teacher, and then as a Headteacher. It mattered then that I made those reports accurate, for the children and their parents. This was like the most important report I'd ever have to write. Now I was being given the opportunity, I was nervous and worried. It would be a great challenge to write a report about a wartime hero, someone who I already felt in awe of and thankful to for what he and his colleagues did before I was even born. If I got it right it would make a huge difference to many people.

How lucky I felt. Luck had already cropped up in Captain Hannaford's unfolding story several times. I had discovered it had been there when he needed it most.

Only a few days later I had the reply from John Hannaford's daughter Jill, saying the family agreed that I could continue. I was delighted. I spent a long time looking at the painting, newly framed and hanging above my writing table and marvelling at my good fortune and wondering where it would lead. I shivered with anticipation.

In that last interview he said he had a 'wonderful life' and a 'wonderful wife'. He'd had an eventful time as a young soldier, as so many had, but the rest of his life had been good. He went on to have a successful career as an architect and a fulfilling life as a husband, father, grandfather and great grandfather. He was an accomplished artist – my initial link to him and the key to my discovery into the past.

I felt I needed to find out about his life before and after his time served as a Bomb Disposal officer. It would help shed light on his story and would help me to understand him better.

I already knew instinctively that the war years of WWII were the ones that he wanted remembered. He spoke of nothing else towards the end of his long life. He repeated it wasn't for him, "but for the men and women of all ranks and in all services who served in the bomb disposal units giving the ultimate sacrifice for their country".

He fervently believed "they were heroes, every one of them."

I already believed he was an unsung hero.

CHAPTER II
FAMILY FORTUNES

A few weeks later I was invited to John and Joyce Hannaford's flat by Jackie and Jill, their daughters. I was shown into a bright room flooded with clear spring sunlight. It was reflecting off the sparkling sea across the road beyond the promenaders and dog walkers, and stretching out to the horizon. Over to the right was the sweeping curve of Pevensey Bay and the Sussex Downs and along to the left the De La Warr Pavilion, Galley Hill and Hastings.

Their home was the perfect place to meet their daughters and start piecing together the information I already had. I was filled with awe to be where John and Joyce had sat so few months before and to go past John's paintings stacked in the corridor was an unusual, surreal moment. What was I doing? I asked myself as I quickly moved past. I wanted to pause and look at them, those results of his peaceful pastime, such a contrast to his wartime occupation that I was starting to find out about.

I was nervous but I was determined to give the family the assurance that I was sincere. I already had great respect for their father and mother. I needn't have worried, as they greeted me warmly. It was to be their last visit to Bexhill and they were just finishing clearing the flat. What luck that I was seeing it almost as it had been.

It must have seemed strange to them that I had found the De La Warr watercolour and traced them. They had hoped someone would appreciate it who lived nearby. They were delighted I loved it. They had also prepared for my visit, each with folders of information. Jill laughed as she presented me with a stack of interesting looking scraps of paper and envelopes with handwritten anecdotes.

'Dad didn't believe in notebooks!' she said.

They seemed like treasures to me. I could see I'd have to get used to John's handwriting to decipher all his notes. There were also some scrapbooks of family history to look at, carefully annotated by him.

I recognised the one from the newspaper photograph and his last interview.

They also gave me some books of Teignmouth, Shaldon and Newton Abbot in Devon where John was born and grew up, and where the family still holidayed. I already knew I'd have to visit. Following his story would be fascinating.

I learnt that morning that the Hannaford family had a rich historical ancestry. John's cousin Dorothy Turcotte from Canada had written a book, which they gave me, about an important and illustrious ancestor. Bishop Peter Mews was the last bishop to fight in armour, and in the 17th century became the Bishop of Winchester Cathedral, where he is buried. She wrote that he was a strong-minded man, willing to act or speak out on any issue. As

I learnt more about John, it was clear that he had inherited some of his ancestor's attributes. Throughout his life and certainly towards the end, John was a man with a mission. He had many strong opinions which he enjoyed sharing and was not averse to complaining about to his family and to the local newspaper. He often dropped in to talk to journalist John Dowling to air his views, especially if he was annoyed about some plan for a new build in the town that he didn't think worthy.

Pilot Tom Hannaford, John's father

Tom, his father and Jill and Jackie's grandfather, was proud of their family links and had a saying, "Riches to rags, rags to riches".

Their ancestors had been powerful and wealthy. He believed that one day that would happen again for his family and future generations of Hannafords. He referred often to Bishop Mews and a few other notable ancestors, one who'd been a mayor. He was a jolly man and he would laugh and say it was their family motto. He instilled in his son the will to make it come true. John said he was born in the 'rags time', but was also confident he could bring the family back to riches after recent hard times.

"Dad called us the four J's," they laughed, as they started to tell me about their father.

The 4 Js - Joyce, Jill, Jackie and John

They didn't know very much about his time in bomb disposal, as he hadn't spoken about it while they were growing up. In fact, one year on November 5th whilst their father was setting off the fireworks, a spark shot into the opened box and the whole lot went up. They made a hasty retreat. It was very funny afterwards, especially when they found out that he had been someone who worked closely with explosives. Not until he retired and started to attend officers' reunions did he share his countless stories of his wartime adventures.

So the family also wanted to learn more and Jill gave me some telephone numbers of family, friends and Royal Engineer contacts. Jackie gave me a folder and photos and shared that John wasn't her biological father. It had been printed in an obituary, I had found out that first afternoon. It had made me feel uncomfortable learning such sensitive family details. It was one of the reasons I wanted their permission to carry on. She explained a little about her mother Joyce and how she had moved back to live with her parents so they could help with the new baby. Sadly, her mother-in-law had not agreed to the marriage and wanted nothing more to do with his wife and her new grandchild after her son's death. Just the day before Jackie had found a photo of her natural father whilst clearing her mother's dressing table drawer. It was the first time she'd seen her father, Bernard Smith.

Two years after the end of the war in 1947 Joyce and John met at a dance in Chiswick. She was still living with her parents and he lived in digs close by. When they married, John adopted Jackie as his own daughter. Then Jill came along. John and Joyce never discussed her first husband with Jackie.

Besides John's handwritten notes, Jill brought along two CDs of an interview by the Imperial War Museum. Jill smiled, saying she thought 'they expected a half-hour talking to a forgetful

95-year-old,' but once warmed up answering questions, John's memory was sharp, and eight hours later his interview concluded. Later when I listened I thought the interviewer's voice became a little weary. It had been a long day but John sounded disappointed at the end and willing to carry on.

John and Joyce

John's training to be an architect began before the war and continued after it ended. He finished his long and distinguished career as Principal Regional Architect for the Property Services Agency, a Government-linked company in the South-East of England. His link with bombs carried on, and throughout the 1950s and early 1960s he worked at Aldermaston nuclear weapons factory in Berkshire, the UK's Atomic Weapons Establishment. The Trident submarine intercontinental ballistic missile system was manufactured there. It was the site of numerous protests. The protestors were the newly formed CND (Campaign for Nuclear Disarmament), started by philosopher Bertrand Russell and Canon John Collins. Many protest marches took place from there to Whitehall and in future years from London to Aldermaston.

John wrote in his notes, "I didn't like it at all."

John Hannaford ARIBA. He had achieved letters after his name. He and his family were so proud. He became an Associate of the Royal Institute of British Architects and he felt his greatest achievement was his last before he retired. He planned the new coastguard's station at Dover in 1978. It is an important building guiding shipping through the busy narrow straits within sight of France – the busiest channel in the world. It is an imaginatively designed building high above the town overlooking the English Channel. It was officially opened by His Royal Highness Prince Charles. The innovative building won awards for its design and was John's pride and joy. He enjoyed telling the story of the day he was presented to Prince Charles who arrived by helicopter. He was a few minutes late as he circled the impressive building atop the cliffs above the town whilst everyone waited below. When he was introduced to John as the architect in charge, Prince Charles congratulated him and told him how well it looked from above. John didn't like to tell him he had arrived from Hastings the day before also by helicopter to get a good aerial view of his building. He already knew how magnificent it looked.

Prince Charles and John

Dover Coastguard Station (courtesy of Croytech)

As I listened to these stories I now understood how his watercolour of the De La Warr showed the understanding of the structure of the building. His skills as a draughtsman were deftly used in the painting, and his accurate ruled lines of the many windows. It was truly a most suitable subject to show off his knowledge as an architect. As Emily told me, his friends had a copy, but I had the original work which gave me great pleasure.

Jill had also brought me a DVD copy of two documentaries about John and his colleagues filmed by Channel 4 called *Danger UXB*. I would later be given the written report from an interview of a first meeting to find out about his suitability for the programme. He passed with flying colours. In fact the interviewer said his descriptions of the workings of bombs were the clearest he'd heard. He also described John "as a bit of a lad!", telling the story of an evening in war-torn London when he had used his Austin pickup (strictly not allowed for socialising) to visit a young lady in Baker Street. The vehicle was parked on the road below. It was spotted by the MP who tried to start it to take it away! But there was a particular way it had been immobilised. Captain Hannaford looked out from the room above, apparently from a horizontal position. He shouted to the officers from the window and hurriedly descended and showed them the secret switch. They had flooded the engine so he couldn't drive it. They towed it back and gave him a lift to the barracks and luckily it went no further. He was not reprimanded, which he was thankful for.

The two documentaries were a wonderful asset. John was in his eighties but looked younger, and was very animated and told his stories with ease and charm. A good talker and raconteur, I wondered why he hadn't written his wartime story himself? Quite a few other Royal Engineer Bomb Disposal specialists had decided to tell their courageous tales. In fact they were sources I used to help me understand how it felt to work in the Royal Engineers in WWII. Thanks to Lieutenant Colonel Eric Wakeling and Major Arthur Hogben I pieced together the wartime world of the bomb disposal officers. Then a presentation by retired Lieutenant Colonel Roderick MacArthur, Commander of 49 Squadron, 1975-1976, Chairman of the Royal Engineers Bomb Disposal Officers Club, put it all into perspective from then until the present day. His presentation showed clearly the drop in figures of Bomb Disposal personnel. After the war the teams were reduced and disbanded, and that is probably why John thought they were being forgotten. But the table of figures also showed clearly how numbers and units were now increasing.

It would have been so good for John to study this, but he and his colleagues are all gone.

After the war the Bomb Disposal teams went their separate ways, building futures and probably trying to forget the bombings and the destruction. Everybody's thoughts were focused on the future, including John Hannaford's. The noises and chaos of war and the celebrations and exhilaration of winning were soon replaced by the sounds of heavy machines clearing away the debris, and men and women returning to work and family life with newfound gusto. New buildings, towns and roads were being erected across the country. There was plenty of work for a young and ambitious architect, and life moved on at a considerable pace.

Royal Engineers Bomb Disposal

Numbers of Personnel

World War II

Date	Men per Section	Sections	Companies	Groups	Total
Nov 1939	3	20			60
May 1940	16	25			400
Jun 1940	16	109			1,700
Jul 1940	16	220	22		4,200
Sep 1940	32	300	24	4	10,000

Notes

1. Total strength includes Company HQ & Group HQ Personnel.
2. Groups are called Regiments today. Some companies were independent, not in Groups.

Post World War II

With the peace came demobilisation and a drastic reduction in all army units. Companies renamed as Squadrons and Sections renamed as Troops.

Date	Regular Squadrons	Reserve (TA) Squadrons	Regiments or equivalent	Totals	
				Regular	Reserve
Apr 1948	9	2	1	1,350	300
Apr 1949	4	2	1	600	300
Jan 1950	1	11	4	150	1,650
Mar 1967	1	1	1	150	150
Jan 1981	1	4	1	150	600
Jan 1983	3	4	2	450	600
Jan 1991	4	4	2	600	600
Jan 1999	5	4	2	750	600
Aug 2018	7	4	3	1,050	600

Notes

1. Numbers are approximate and include civilian personnel in Regular and Reserve Units.
2. January 1950 – Reduced to equivalent of one regular BD Squadron. Three Army Emergency Reserve (TA) Regiments (total of 9 Squadrons) formed, but disbanded in March 1967.
3. 1969 – Title EOD (Explosive Ordnance Disposal) replaced BB (Bomb Disposal).
4. 1973 - HQ EOD Units RE renamed as 33 Engineer Regiment (EOD), with one regular Squadron, one TA Squadron and a Tri-Service EOD School. Three more TA squadrons formed by 1981.
5. 1983 – following Falklands War in 1982 two more regular EOD Squadrons formed, and the four TA Squadrons reorganised into a separate Regiment, 101 Engineer Regiment (EOD).
6. 1991 – Fourth Regular EOD Squadron formed following Gulf War.
7. By 1999 – Fifth Regular EOD Squadron formed due to Balkans.
8. 2018 reorganisation will create a third RE EOD regiment and two more regular squadrons.

I had a lot of research to do. I still couldn't quite believe what was happening but I was pleased to be finding out about John Hannaford's family from John's daughters. I hadn't had the opportunity to meet him, but I had the great good fortune of meeting them and having their support. Looking at his notes and the pile of books, I had the next best thing. There was much to do and I was itching to get started. Naïvely I thought it would be done by the end of the year, but John's story deserved to take considerably longer in order to follow all his leads. In fact, it took two more years of research, meetings, travel and discovery before any conclusions started to form.

The next morning I had a message from Jill saying they had another book that might be useful for my research. When I got there they surprised me by presenting me with two more paintings. One was of actress Ellen Terry's house not far away in Tenterden, and the other of St Mark's in Venice, where my husband and I had spent our honeymoon so it has special significance for us. It had that same architectural style I liked so much in the De La Warr Pavilion painting, but more detailed to highlight that beautiful building, and it showed again that architect's understanding of structure and perspective and John's love of light and shadow. I was touched by their generosity and thanked them.

As I left, Jackie and Jill told me they had just scattered the ashes of their mother and father at their favourite spot by the sea. It was good to hear they were still together and in a place they loved.

CHAPTER III
GROWING UP

John told many people that he was a very lucky man but he was born in WWI at a time of great upheaval and uncertainty, and his young family were surrounded by broken families with their menfolk away fighting a bloody battle abroad or, worse still, not returning home at the end of it. It was not unknown even in their small community for fathers, brothers and sons from the same family all to be killed. Luckily his father Tom was based in Aldershot, firstly as a mechanic, then training and becoming a pilot. Though John's mother was on her own, there were family nearby to help. They were not poor, but it was still a struggle to survive those difficult times.

John's association with bombs started early in WWI, not many months after his birth.

One evening after he'd been taken to visit his grandmother in London, his mother was pushing him in his pram along the Embankment. It was a warm summer's night in early September 1917. His mother looked up and saw some planes. The late evening walk to settle him had the opposite effect. Night bombings were unheard of at the time. The planes that came overhead were the first aerial bombardment in the heart of the capital. At first no one realised what was about to occur. In fact the crowds along the Thames stared skyward, wondering what was happening. The searchlights picked up the planes, then someone shouted to run for cover. There was panic. People ran to get under bridges and hide wherever they could. There was confusion and disbelief followed by great explosions and people screaming and acrid smoke filling the air. Baby John would surely have cried as his mother dashed with him to safety.

The bombs were aiming for Charing Cross station, but missed. A tram was hit, killing the conductor and two passengers, and leaving a huge hole in the road, exposing the underground railway below. The bomb which exploded nearest to them scattered shrapnel into the statue of the Sphinx, narrowly missing them and Cleopatra's Needle. You can still see the pockmarks to this day splattered over the plinth of the Sphinx with holes ripped into the metal paws of the great beast. In his interview for the Imperial War Museum John would wryly recall this early link and narrow escape.

In 2008 John wrote: 'Unbelievably saw for the first time an aerial photo from a German bomber in 1917 dropping bombs on London. One clearly on the Embankment and confirmed the story from my mother that we, with me in the pram, were very close to that bomb.'

Sphinx bomb damage 1917

Heavy Gotha Bomber, England Squadron 1917. Courtesy of the BBC

Earlier in the war Zeppelins had dropped bombs elsewhere, mostly targeting the docks, but they were unreliable and didn't always hit their targets. Dover and Kent had been hit, resulting in over 200 casualties. That night in September 1917, five new heavy Gotha bombers, designed to fly further, headed up the Thames. They carried more bombs and were able to drop their load of bombs more accurately. They reached right to the heart of the city and unleashed a new kind of warfare on London and its people who were unprepared. After the shock and horror the Government started a building programme for shelters. They would become better used in the Blitz in WWII and save many lives.

John's mother Amy stayed clear of Central London after that frightening experience, but she would often talk about their narrow escape and unhappily how her son went back to those close shaves with enemy bombs as a young officer in the next war.

Following the euphoria of the end of WWI, the country experienced an unsteady peace. The cost of the Great War was immense and governments were heavily in debt to rich countries such as the USA, our country included. But there was optimism, which led to the exciting and innovative years in which John grew up. John's parents had a strong partnership and that stability allowed him to enjoy his early experiences before the country descended into the Depression and the economic slump of the 30s.

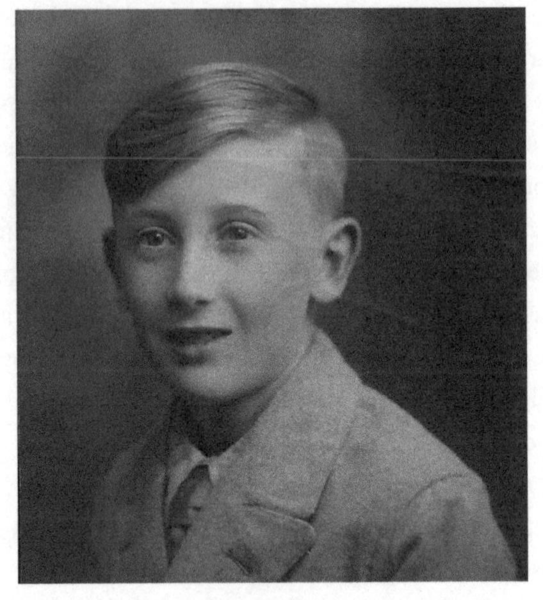

Young John

John's father, Tom Hannaford, was a returning hero and one of the first pilots to fly an Avro plane in WWI and he'd named his son after that plane: Avro Frederick John Hannaford. He was sure it would be a name for his son to be proud of. Not so! It was never a popular choice with his son, who soon chose to be called John. He came to that conclusion after receiving his first-ever letter addressed to 'Miss Avro Hannaford'. He was disgusted, even writing to the letters page of his newspaper, *The Daily Telegraph*, many years later when the subject of unusual names relating to aircraft arose. There had also been some name-calling at school. He didn't take kindly to being called Avril. It must have made him more resilient. He also had a quick wit to get out of difficult situations and had inherited his father's sense of humour. He could stand up for himself, but changing his name avoided the problem.

John was lucky to be born in one of the most green and pleasant places in England, near the beautiful estuary of the River Teign in Devon. He played outdoors in the park near his home and often went to swim and sail, and learnt to fish in the sheltered estuary of the Teign. As he later described it, he enjoyed a 'free-range' childhood with space to grow, explore and learn. It was a happy childhood, full of opportunities and adventure. He also had a talent for art, which got him noticed in school. The resulting opportunities he was then given shaped his whole life and assured him of that rich future sought after by his father Tom. He attended school in Newton Abbot where he could remember many poor children who went to school without shoes. He knew his family struggled to make ends meet, but he always had shoes.

Even though women over 30 had been given the vote in 1918 John was still luckier to be born a male. He was the treasured son of a family where they recognised the value of education in order to fulfil any ambition for a brighter future. He was given every opportunity to develop his skills and talents. The changes for women were not quick enough for his elder sister Lola, who had aspirations to train as a hairdresser but wasn't given those same opportunities.

Tragedy hit the family. His younger sister Pat died of meningitis. She was only three years old and three years younger than John. Fortunately he remained healthy. But it was he who was given the daunting task of going to fetch his big sister Lola who was out with a friend, and he had to give her the terrible news. She and the family were devastated. He remembered his father crying but he said it didn't seem to affect him so deeply. Later he told his niece he regretted he hadn't been closer to her mother Lola.

John was an able scholar and attended Wolborough Boys School, then the Technical College in Newton Abbot. He won first prize in a national competition for a sketch he did at the local art college. His headmaster had spotted his artistic talents and knew the principal, and managed to get him a day release there each week. Later he also arranged for John to join as an apprentice to the only man with letters after his name in Newton Abbot, the established architect Josias C. Beare ARIBA ARCA. The recession was a time of great poverty, with few job opportunities, so it was a real stroke of luck for young John.

John's first position as apprentice architect for Josias C Beare ARIBA, ARCA

Josias Beare was an artist as well as an architect who had an exemplary reputation and made a great impression on young John. He gave him his foundation of knowledge as an apprentice architect and paved the way for a good and profitable future. It was with his support and connections that John managed to gain his next apprenticeship with His Majesty's Ministry of Works in Whitehall.

He had an aunt and uncle who lived in a flat in the Strand where he stayed at first, and which allowed him to walk to work and at the same time get his bearings. Later he found digs in Kennington Park. They introduced him to the best places in London and took him to shows and the cinema. He explored and found his way around on the trams – two old pence a ride, he remembered – and he could get all the way to Woolwich.

Me and My Girl was a hot ticket at the theatre, and the song 'The Lambeth Walk' a great hit. Judy Garland was singing her hit, 'Somewhere Over the Rainbow'. It was *Top Hat* that everyone was talking about, with Fred Astaire and Ginger Rogers as the most stunning dancing and singing partnership the world had ever seen. Hollywood sparkled on the big screen even in black and white. It was so uplifting, a real feel-good film and great escapism. You came out of the cinema tapping your feet, and John soon learnt to dance. Dance halls were everywhere in the city. It was a place for young people to meet up. Everyone wanted to learn all the new crazes of dancing, copying the swing and quickstep of *Top Hat*. The influence of the Deep South of America's jazz era was also fast becoming the fun and exhilarating new style of dance, encouraging a freedom that unsettled older folk. But with war on the horizon it was hard to forget the slaughter of a whole generation of young people only 20 years before. Those old enough to remember recognised a need for the young to find an outlet for their energy, so there was also generally an acceptance of their high spirits.

John said, "The city was alive and a thrilling place to be working." He was just 20 but his confidence had grown and he was ready for any adventure that would come his way. His aunt was more cautious and warned him which areas to steer clear of. There had been trouble in the East End of London a few months before he arrived in the capital. The Battle of Cable Street, as it was named, had seen fighting between the Fascists and Blackshirts, supporters of politician Oswald Mosley, and the Jewish community and other groups opposing them and standing up to their bullying ways. The clash in October 1936 involved the police who were protecting the march and trying to keep the peace. The majority of both marchers and protesters travelled into the area to confront each other. The community remained nervous and tension continued, but many had moved away from the area afterwards. Still, John took note of his aunt's warnings and stayed clear.

London struck John as very modern in comparison with sleepy Devon. But he didn't like the foggy days. The smog shocked him. He had never realised how clean and fresh the air was in Devon. But he was overjoyed with the advances in technology he witnessed. London was still ablaze with lights before the wartime blackout, especially around the theatres in Covent Garden and the West End with their glitz and flashing attractions. He couldn't wait to own his first car: they were everywhere, adding to the excitement and the hustle and bustle of the great city. Along with the double-deckers advertising each new film they competed with the trams on the busy roads. The noise was sometimes deafening but also exciting. His dad had taught him to drive earlier in his teens, but even the market day in Newton Abbot was a far cry from Piccadilly Circus. It would remain a love of his life. He drove his car well into his nineties.

There were new red telephone boxes in all the public places and for the first time you could ring 999 if you needed help from police, fire brigade or ambulance, and you could also call up the speaking clock to check the time.

John's engaging voice was well modulated and rich, the burr of a West Country accent hardly discernible. He enjoyed talking and telling a good joke and recounting a funny story, and he already had many experiences to draw upon.

Though short in stature he was charismatic and charming, described by others as eloquent and later as 'a true gentleman'. His fair hair was combed back and he sported a neat little moustache. He dressed smartly and enjoyed wearing a hat, and later in life would greet others by tipping it at a jaunty angle. Of course, there are two sides to every coin and John could also be quite agitated, irritated and annoyed, and didn't suffer fools gladly. You might say he had a short fuse! He was once described as someone who "called a spade a shovel".

John had grown up through changing times and nothing fazed him. As a young apprentice architect he believed the family motto was changing in his favour and felt he was improving himself greatly. He earned a good salary of £2 5s per week, and after paying board and lodgings he had some funds left over to save and some to go out enjoying himself. Moving to the city he felt close to the heart of things.

The love affair of Prince Edward and Mrs Simpson had rocked the royal family to its foundations and had filled the country's newspapers. It was a constant topic of conversation and took their minds off the threat of another war. King Edward was popular with the people, and as Prince of Wales had represented his father King George V, travelling through the Commonwealth and meeting many people around the country.

He had many supporters but his reign was short. He was only monarch from the 20th January until the 11th December 1936. Edward voluntarily abdicated when his advisors told him he would not be allowed to marry the twice-divorced Wallis Simpson because of his position as Head of the Church of England. By the time John arrived in London everyone knew there was to be a new king crowned: his brother would become King George VI.

'London was a frantic place,' John said, 'full of preparations, edgy, still at peace, but no one knew for how long.'

What a year to arrive in London. In 1937 there was an air of expectation. The Prime Minister of the national coalition was Stanley Baldwin, but only until the end of May. He was exhausted after the abdication following the royal scandal. He retired. Neville Chamberlain took over. His would be a different nightmare of a job. Nothing like it had happened before. The Government had been adamant that our king could not marry a divorced woman. It had to look closely at the Constitution and strengthen the monarchy in the face of war, and be sure their decision to support the new king and queen was well received by the public. Indeed the new king needed much support. He was a reluctant monarch who had to overcome his own difficulties and learn to speak without his stammer interrupting his speeches. But they needn't have worried: Britain looked forward to the coronation. The new King George and Queen Elizabeth-to-be and their young daughters Elizabeth and Margaret Rose were already popular.

John's first job was in preparation for the coronation of King George VI. He walked to his office in Whitehall or to Westminster as the chimes of Big Ben struck, and then home again along the busy Strand. The excitement was palpable. The city started to take on a party atmosphere. There were flags fluttering all the way down The Mall and souvenirs and photos of the new royals everywhere. Everyone felt patriotic and hopeful. After the uncertainty of the newly named Duke of Windsor's refusal to abandon Mrs Simpson for the Crown, there was a great sense of relief. The public didn't like photographs of the Duke and Duchess of Windsor in Germany meeting their leaders, including Adolf Hitler. But the preparations for the new coronation blocked out the gloomy news from the continent of the upsurge of Hitler and Nazism. They were momentarily forgotten.

John and his young colleagues spent three months surveying the interior of Westminster Abbey so that the tiers of galleries for seating could be constructed for the congregation and the great coronation ceremony to come, to be filled with royalty, Government and dignitaries from the Commonwealth and other countries around the world.

1,000 tons of steel were used. He felt on top of the world: few of his friends had even been to London, let alone been involved in such a magnificent national and world event. It was the first coronation to be filmed by the BBC. It would appear in cinemas across the country so that everyone could witness the pomp and splendour of the occasion.

King George VI sitting on the Coronation seat where John had sat
Courtesy of the BBC

One morning when the Dean went out and left them to it, they were feeling full of confidence and bravado, and his young colleague made a paper crown and dared him to sit on the Coronation Chair with the Stone of Scone underneath, which he did, and there Avro Frederick John Hannaford of Shaldon in the county of Devon was crowned King John of England. It was a hilarious but rather daring and risky prank. Luckily, no one discovered the play-acting.

But it wasn't all fun and joking. The architect in overall charge based his design of the Annexe using the drawings of the 1902 coronation of King George V. John was despatched one day to plot the external trees, and when he took the details back, the architect was, in John's words, 'stunned and literally went white'. The 1937 Annexe was much larger than the previous and therefore the tree, a very large one, appeared precisely in the centre of The Queen's Robing Room. The Dean refused to have the tree cut down and, as plans had already been approved by all up to the King and Queen-to-be, via the Earl Marshal, the Duke of Norfolk, panic set in. The architect was sacked. Fortunately, another solution was found and the offending tree is still living and flourishing today.

As a result of his work on the design John was given the job of steward on a stand with a prime position outside the gates of Buckingham Palace. He was able to invite his parents from Devon. They stood cheering and waving flags all day. He was positioned close by and shared the excitement.

John and his mother and father watched the newly crowned King George VI, Queen Elizabeth and Princesses Elizabeth and Margaret on the balcony at Buckingham Palace

The Princesses Elizabeth and Margaret waved to them as they processed past in their open carriages, bedecked in rich colour, fine jewels and ermine robes. They were well positioned in the throng looking up to the balcony afterwards as the Royal party appeared. There was cheering and calls of 'Long live the King'. It was a truly memorable and exciting day. John kept his steward's badge as a memento and shared the story of his part in the new king's coronation, and his own paper coronation, many times. He always enjoyed telling the story and could hear his father saying, 'Riches to rags, rags to riches'. Family fortunes were beginning to work for him, but not even his father had envisaged a coronation in the family. It always made him chuckle and raised a laugh at his audacity as a young apprentice architect.

CHAPTER IV
PREPARATION AND WAR

John's link with bombs continued as he became directly involved in the mass preparation for war. He and a team of architects and planners were relocated many miles north in Lancashire at the Royal Ordnance Filling Factory at Chorley. It became known as the No 1. Filling Factory in the country, the biggest munitions filling site. It was an offshoot of the Royal Arsenal in Woolwich, but Chorley was 220 miles from London, hidden away and safer from enemy bombing raids. John missed being in the city but he loved the new job, his team of workmates in the planning department and their important war work. It was a hive of activity, an important place to be for the war effort, and when finished it was officially opened by King George VI himself.

John described that the three processes of making shells, producing explosive chemicals and then filling them, followed by priming the shells ready for use, were all kept a safe distance apart. The shell casings were often made in cotton mills or iron foundries nearby.

The chemicals used for the explosives were made by separate chemical companies, and the explosives were placed well away from cities and towns with a good rail link to the filling factory. ROF Chorley had its own private railway station. The dangerous work of filling and priming the shells with the explosives was completed at ROF Chorley.

Gracie Fields at Chorley

John spent two years working there in the planning office as the building was constructed on the immense site. His team were very aware of the danger and volatility of the processes to be carried out. Safety considerations were paramount. The design, style and spacing of individual production buildings meant that they were separated by wide, open spaces. Depending on the work being carried out, there were approximately six-metre-high, grassed embankments with thick, reinforced concrete walls and overbridges. These were built to deflect any explosion skyward, rather than outward to any adjacent buildings or structures. The site was built with extensive underground magazines. One day John remembered seeing a man sitting on a ladder polishing the pointed end of a huge bomb. He said it was surreal.

There were also comprehensive lightning protection and individual buildings linked by paths, roads and railways. John could remember curved entrances where the highly volatile chemicals were used, and a scientist working there told him he used a mirror to work around corners from a distance and that even the touch of a feather could cause the materials to explode. The components were lead azide, fulminate mercury, RDX and TNT, the most dangerous explosives most widely used in WWII.

The vast, 928-acre site had a 9-mile perimeter fence and was heavily guarded with massive, 6-metre-high brick boundary walls around the railway station. As a further safety precaution there were separate entrances to the explosives site. There was an administration site and a larger area of the site divided by the railway line that was the main explosives filling site.

It had its own fire station, police station and medical centre. John said the management took great pride in looking after its workforce. There was a canteen for workers equipped with a stage that was used for concerts and other entertainment. Whilst he was there he enjoyed a lively social scene with dances, competitions and concerts. John's favourite entertainer who came to perform was Gracie Fields. 'She was wonderful,' he said. She sang all her popular hits, 'Sally', 'Falling in Love Again' and 'Sing As We Go', which they all joined in with. Her funny songs like 'The Biggest Aspidistra in the World' and 'I Took My Harp to a Party' were hilarious and everyone cheered her. Her laughing as much as her singing was a great morale booster for John and his friends.

Work continued night and day and John remembered being

amazed to find that a road had been built outside his window overnight. Attention to detail was ever-present, which suited John who was trained in detailed and precise technical drawing skills, which were measured to the minutest detail for planning. His patience and tenacity showed through in his carefully executed drawings. All of these skills and experiences were to come in very handy, sooner rather than later. He enjoyed the company of his team, young men caught up in wartime preparations like him. They were all trying to live in the moment, not thinking too far into the uncertain future.

John seated with his team of workmates in the Drawing Office

Aerial photo of ROF, Chorley

Filling Bombs at ROF, Chorley

Even before ROF Chorley was finished it was realised that it would not have the necessary capacity to meet Britain and the Commonwealth's needs for ammunition. In all, some 20 Government-owned filling factories were built, but none was as large or employed as many people as Chorley. The new factory employed over 1,000 production workers by the outbreak of the WWII. By June 1940, the numbers employed there had risen to nearly 15,000, and at its wartime peak ROF Chorley had over 28,000 employees. John heard that the cost of the plant was £13,140,000. He said, 'It was a staggering amount then.'

On holiday in Italy days before the outbreak of WWII

Although Europe was on the brink of years of war in the summer of 1939 he had just returned from the South of France and Italy. He'd driven down with friends. France was friendly and not expecting to be invaded as soon as it was. To some it might seem a foolhardy thing to do: it was certainly an adventure. His holiday photo looks as though he and his friends had a great time with no hint of imminent war. Their carefree smiles, together with the pretty girls holding bouquets of fresh flowers, show how they were enjoying themselves. It looked great fun. The news that filtered through to them and that they heard from the locals wasn't good, but the warm sunshine and the welcoming holiday atmosphere on the Mediterranean coast and in Ventimiglia, where their photo was taken, gave them a brief respite.

Though everyone was trying to be upbeat, especially young people like John, the determined marching of the Nazis reported across Europe and into Poland was a sinister message that couldn't be ignored. To return to gloomy London with its sandbags stacked up by the side of the roads and the blacked-out and taped windows brought him back to reality and down to earth. In the gardens they passed they could see the corrugated-steel Anderson shelters already erected and signs directed others to use the crowded public shelters. In late 1940, Morrison shelters were introduced, which were not much more than a steel table with angled, thick iron legs to hide under, inside your home, and there were instances when the house had collapsed around the family but they remained safe below the steel table.

The whole nation listened to the BBC radio broadcast by Prime Minister Neville Chamberlain that first Sunday in September. He spoke in very sombre tones:

'I am speaking to you from the Cabinet Room of 10 Downing Street. This morning the British Ambassador in Berlin handed the German Government a final note, stating that unless we heard from them – by 11 o'clock – that they were prepared at once to withdraw their troops from Poland, a state of war would exist between us. I have to tell you now that no such undertaking has been received and that, consequently, this country is at war with Germany.'

Tensions had been mounting for some time as everyone waited and hoped for some solution that might prevent war even at that last moment. They were still digesting the news, frozen in the moment, when the wailing sirens went off right after the announcement and the mass of barrage balloons that John saw went up into the sky to snare enemy planes. People piled out of buildings into air-raid shelters. The declaration of war wasn't a surprise, as there had been regular updates on the radio and in cinemas, but still hearing the sirens panicked everyone.

A later broadcast from King George VI also called upon them to be strong:

'My people at home and my peoples across the seas…to stand calm, firm and united in this time of trial. The task will be hard. There may be dark days ahead and war can no longer be confined to the battlefield. But we can only do the right as we see the right and reverently commit our cause to God.'

'No longer be confined to the battlefield' was indeed a warning for all the population, both in the Commonwealth and in Britain. Everyone would be affected. No previous war would compare to what was to come.

That evening John met his cousin at the flat in the Strand. Whilst his aunt was out, they talked long into the night about their hopes and fears for themselves, their families and the country. They'd seen a lot of newsreels and propaganda already:

there were posters plastered everywhere about spies and 'careless talk' costing lives. In the privacy of his aunt's flat they were sharing views they couldn't openly discuss at work or even with their friends.

John said, 'My cousin was to join the RAF and pilot planes and go up in the air; I was to join the RE Bomb Disposal and go down into the ground.'

It was a wary and fearful nation that night that took in a deep breath and waited for war to begin. However, it didn't, and nor did it for some months.

John returned to ROF Chorley. The phoney war had begun. They spent months listening to the news of the Nazi onslaught. As 1940 dawned, Britain was four months into the second war against Germany in barely more than 20 years. But so far there had been little action on the Home Front. Evacuees began to drift back home and people grumbled about wartime measures that seemed to have no point.

Ebbw Vale MP Aneurin Bevan told Parliament: 'the impression is now universal that if the Germans do not manage to bomb us to death the Ministry of Information will bore us to death.'

But the Government continued to send out the messages. Britain prepared.

By the start of 1940, 44 million gas masks had been distributed and everyone had to carry one or more if you had children and babies in prams.

The sound of Adolf Hitler ranting became a familiar soundtrack accompanying the German Army relentlessly marching towards the Channel. The cinemas were packed as newsreels showed maps with giant arrows indicating the strength of the German assault crushing neighbouring countries. On the radio the voice of Lord Haw-Haw, an American-born Irish Fascist who became a German citizen in 1940, broadcast propaganda throughout the war. The first fake news broadcaster! He mocked us as he spread bad or false news to try to undermine morale.

After the swift and unexpected fall of France, the nature of the war changed. Suddenly Britain was standing alone and the enemy was just a few miles away across the English Channel. The bombing of British towns and cities began, concentrated on London but extending across much of the country.

John enlisted in October 1939 and waited to hear where he would be posted. Finally he received his call-up papers whilst still working at Chorley on the 5th March 1940.

He had wondered about trying for the RAF like his father and cousin, but was told that they were only recruiting rear gunners, not pilots. Everyone knew they only had a 16-week life expectancy. So he decided on the Royal Engineers.

He wrote: 'Nice safe job, I thought.' His letter was addressed to Sapper Hannaford 7724249, telling him to report to Trafford Park to 567 Company Royal Engineers.

Another of John's notes said: 'That sounded good.' That was also wrong.

He envisaged a stately home with green acres surrounding the grandeur of the building. But he was to be very disappointed. He had to delay his journey there for two weeks, as he was ill, so when he finally got to the nearby railway station he decided to get a taxi. It was a wrong move, he wrote later. As he stepped from the taxi the 300 or so sappers, mostly sons of dockers from Liverpool, thought he must be someone important. He really got a ribbing when they found out he was just another sapper arriving for training like them. And later it got even worse when they saw him take out his neatly folded pyjamas, which his mother had carefully put in his pack, and lay them on his bed. Most of them wore nothing at all in bed and nobody else seemed to own a pair of pyjamas. They were a rough lot and it took John a while to live it down, but when he described those men later he could only praise them. 'They were salt of the earth,' he said.

Trafford Park was an abandoned stately home, once owned by the oldest and most noble family in the area. By the time the Royal Engineers arrived it was completely run-down with no electricity or power. It was grim. Rooms were dirty and full of pigeon muck and filth. The businessman to whom it was sold in 1896, Ernest Terah Hooley, surrounded it with the first industrial estate in the world, without ever renovating the main house. Where the deer park had been there was every imaginable factory or industry, including the Ford car company.

'We practised drilling to make us soldiers,' John wrote. The Royal Engineers training was all about marching, drilling and teamwork. Describing it to the IWM interviewer he said: 'The only place we could parade was up and down a road flanked by ugly little factories chucking out all sorts of smoke and fumes. As we marched, the brass badges on our hats changed colour with the pollution.' He described it as a foul and appalling place.

They also learnt to dig trenches. John was skilled at holding a pencil, but according to him no good at all at wielding a shovel.

'I was a terrible wimp,' he said. 'After turning over a couple of clumps of earth I offered another chap half a crown to dig for me.' He laughed as he said: 'I was learning how to survive in the Army.'

John in his Austin 7

John was soon promoted to lance corporal and given his own car, an Austin 7 open-top, which he adored. His speedy promotion he felt fairly sure was because he'd written the letter of apology to the major when he was delayed due to illness. His education was paying off. Not many of the sappers seemed to be able to write well. John liked to write: he enjoyed words and expressed himself clearly. His new job was to report back to the major, and he knew he was able to describe accurately the various locations he was sent to. His sketches helped, too. The major was impressed.

They were sent from Manchester to Cardiff and up the Wye Valley, building embankments and trenches with sandbags for trench warfare, preparing the land for invasion. John's job was to go ahead, survey and make drawings of places in a 10-mile radius. He enjoyed the freedom he had in his Austin. It didn't last long, though, as one day the major called him in and said he was sorry but he had to take back the car. Could John ride a motorbike? John hid his disappointment and said he couldn't, so was sent for a lesson in Ross-on-Wye railway station car park from a gruff old sergeant who demonstrated briefly by doing a quick circuit and then got off and shouted, 'Sit on there, Hannaford,' and gave him a few instructions, then 'Off you go.' John wiggled his way around and that was it. The sergeant said, 'You are now an experienced motorcyclist.'

They slept rough in various places along the way. They were building roads and doing some primitive engineering. It was hard, physical work. It was obvious the Government were preparing them all for imminent enemy invasion.

With ever more depressing news about the number of troops already lost in the war John described, 'Panic and chaos everywhere.'

Next, their unit was sent to Tramway Road barracks in December 1940, which was across the Mersey at New Brighton. It was very cold and dark and just before Christmas.

At 6.15 whilst they were having tea they heard the sirens go off which was not unusual, but that night they were followed by the sound of the anti-aircraft or 'Ack-Ack' guns, as everyone called them. A dozen of the guns had been placed on the promenade. They heard the drone of the enemy planes, wave after wave of them, and then bombs started to rain down and explode on

Liverpool Docks and the city until 6.00 the following morning. The sky lit up red with the flames as the docks blazed. There was utter devastation. Though several miles away, they could hear the crackling of the fires. The oil tanks and sugar stores were exploding and on fire, and they could smell the sweet and acrid fumes at the back of their throats. They had hardly recovered when it happened again. The sirens went off the following night and from 6.00 pm until 6.00 am the bombing continued but this time there were no 'Ack-Ack' guns firing back. The next day whilst driving past, John saw their muzzles had peeled back like bananas from the heat generated and the repeated firing. They were rendered useless. The metal had just melted away. Liverpool had been wide open to the enemy bombers and unable to defend itself.

John and his unit were in slip trenches in front of a big house and they'd been there hours watching searchlights criss-crossing the night sky and listening to the drone of planes going over dropping their loads and then seeing incendiary bombs shaped like bottles clattering onto roofs all around them, burning with white-hot flashes of light.

It was cold and John said he went up to his room to put on more clothes. Bombs were coming closer and suddenly he heard what sounded like 'a bus coming down'.

His window, which was covered in tarred paper for the blackout, was blown in. Through the hole where his window had been he saw the big house down the road receive a direct hit. It lifted its roof clean off and the whole building rose into the air. There were sparks, flames and debris everywhere. The house was completely demolished. John later found out that tragically the entire family who had been hiding under the stairs were killed. He described it as 'a hellish nightmare and a close shave'.

He believed it was one of the heaviest raids ever in the UK and after his near miss in WWI London his second encounter with a bombing raid, but this time he was well aware of what was going on. The great northern city of Liverpool was stunned and shocked and pounded into the ground.

The next day, John and his men as Army Troops Company were called upon to help in any way they could. There was no order: John described people 'mooning' about. There was rubble and utter devastation everywhere. His troop were shoring up buildings and making them safe and all the while calling out, then stopping and listening for any voices, for anyone trapped. Shocked people were looking for their families and friends. For John's troop it was a horrendous task as bodies were removed. It was the first time John and many of his men had seen such fatalities, and they were all as shaken and shocked as the population of Liverpool.

It was dangerous clearing the rubble, with power cables and gas pipes broken and there were shards of glass and sharp metal torn and ripped about. It was there that John had his first encounter with a UXB and tragically learnt the danger of an unexploded device. Not all bombs went off. You expected a bomb to explode, but one that didn't was much worse. You had to take even more care and bring in the specialists to help when possible. Instructions at the beginning of the war were scanty. There were few experts. The police and Home Guard were the first to be tasked with the job of clearing bombed sites and UXBs. There was little advice. This was a new type of deadly warfare here on the Home Front.

One of John's men – he described him as 'a nice young chap' – was across the road at a church and had spotted an incendiary bomb sticking out of the flower bed. They were instructed to throw earth on them. Before he could do as directed, the vicar's wife rushed out with a bucket of water and doused the bomb. It exploded with a bang, with white-hot flames shooting up into the young soldier's face, blinding him. He was John's first casualty of the war as lance corporal and he was shocked. 'It broke my heart,' he said. 'Stupid war.'

It seemed not long afterwards that the major called him into his office and told him he had been put forward for a commission. He was sent to Chester and then onto Aldershot to Number 22 Company for six months' training in early 1941.

On his way to Chester he travelled by train and decided to upgrade to a first-class ticket to celebrate becoming an officer. It was an eight-seater compartment and an elderly man was already sitting in a corner. They chatted away and John was proud to share his news about going to train to be an officer. The gentleman congratulated him and they talked throughout the few hours of their journey. When the train stopped at Chester the elderly man also got off and an Army driver approached the man and he heard him say, 'Your car is this way, sir.'

He offered John a lift to the barracks. John discovered he was a retired general also travelling to the officers' training barracks, no doubt to share his expertise. John enjoyed telling the story and chuckling away to himself thinking about how the general listened to his enthusiastic banter, naïve comments and observations, and never let on. He never met him again but he never forgot him either. It wasn't to be the last time he would have interesting conversations with generals. Eventually his war would ensure he had some close encounters with top Royal Engineer generals, but not the kindly gentleman on the train.

At Chester they learnt all about engineering and becoming an officer. There were courses on mechanical and structural engineering and fieldcraft and on how to run a company and even how to give a lecture and instruct your men, to train and keep up morale.

Afterwards at Aldershot he stayed at Malta Barracks which was next to Farnborough where his father had been stationed in WWI. He was pleased he was able to visit. When asked he jumped at the chance to fly in an Avro plane, after which he was named and which his father had piloted. Although proud of his father and his achievements as one of the first WWI pilots, he was still pleased he'd changed his name to John.

He described these early training experiences in war-torn Britain as 'having my eyes wide open all the time'.

He tried to take it all in he said. He knew his future would depend on remembering all the information. He wanted to be the best officer he could be. It was an exciting prospect, he said: 'an adventure'.

John and the other young officers were then sent to a holding battalion at Clitheroe to wait for the War Department to decide about their postings. After morning drill you waited for the lists to go up on the noticeboard to see if your name was there. John was increasingly hopeful, as he saw one fellow officer get his posting to the West Indies to open a water plant.

'Not a bad number,' everyone agreed and patted him on the back.

Another was sent to build a road network in South Africa. John congratulated the officer, agreeing it would be a fine adventure. Finally, the day came and there was his name, and beside it, his posting to Number 16 Bomb Disposal Company, Llandaff, Cardiff, in South Wales. There were a few mutterings and then some reassuring remarks. John had heard the saying, 'Join the Army to see the world. Join Bomb Disposal and see the next one.'

He responded as cheerfully as he could. He was determined to stay positive and later said he felt proud to be doing something so important and a job that was both essential and worthwhile. There was a growing problem of UXBs affecting the whole country as the German bombers continued to pound cities and docks every day and night.

How to deal with the terrifying new threat of UXBs was increasingly in everyone's conversation and in the papers, but Winston Churchill soon stopped news coverage. He thought too much information about the destruction caused by the bombs would find its way back to the enemy. It became top secret. Even after the war John and his bomb disposal colleagues didn't talk about their courageous role in saving so many people, and their homes and livelihoods.

Churchill's ban was only lifted to publicise the amazing story of St Paul's Cathedral's lucky escape from a massive UXB that had burrowed 30 feet under the foundations in Dean's Yard. It was a great morale booster to war-weary Londoners and the rest of the country already suffering the heavy bombing raids. They needed heroes. The newspapers responded.

The Germans had tried and tried to blast the dome of St Paul's to smithereens. St Paul's had its own firewatchers ready to douse any flames.

The iconic building still stood in the very heart of London, even after the heavy bombardment of the Blitz. Its beautifully designed dome towered high above the city surrounded by blasted buildings and rubble on all sides. It showed the enemy a resolute and resilient Britain. The Government used it as a symbol of strength and determination showing the British bulldog spirit.

St Pauls, a symbol of our steadfastness in the Blitz

John saw the photos and articles all over the newspapers with the headline, 'St Paul's Saved'. The heroic tale had been front-page news. Like everyone, John was enthralled to read about this new terror that came from the air. It was real propaganda and some might say perhaps some of the first fake news. It was disputed that the officer in charge, Lieutenant Davies, carried out the defuzing of the bomb. Some said it was Sapper Wyllie. Whatever happened, St Paul's had a narrow escape and survived.

Captain John Hannaford was to read the following report for the 75th Commemoration Service at St Paul's Cathedral in October 2015, a month before he died. He was to be presented to His Royal Highness Prince Harry, and he was to read the report, but due to illness Colonel Mike Brooks OBE, President of the Bomb Disposal branch of the Royal Engineers Association, read it. Jill Buch and John's granddaughter Chloe represented him.

On the morning of Thursday 12th September 1940, Lieutenant Bob Davies of the Royal Engineers received an urgent call. A bomb was heard to fall at about 02.30 hours near the front of St Paul's Cathedral. Since it had not yet detonated there was a suspicion that it may contain a time delay fuze. This was a Category A task: it must be dealt with before it exploded, whatever the cost to human life.

When Lieutenant Davies arrived at St Paul's he saw that a wide space at the front of the steps had already been cordoned off. Judging by the hole in Dean's Yard the bomb was evidently large and had narrowly missed the South West Tower before burying itself a few yards from the cathedral's foundations.

A scan of the scene revealed how potentially damaging the bomb could be. Not only did the angle of impact suggest that it must have burrowed towards the magnificent West front of Wren's masterpiece, but it had also landed atop the entire trunk telephone network to the North of England. If it was a time delay fuze then it had already been ticking for twelve hours out of an accepted maximum of 80.

Time was all-important, and the six sappers working with Lieutenant Davies jumped into the crater and began to chip away at the paving slabs. In a matter of seconds they all went down like skittles, unconscious. The unexploded bomb had fractured a six-inch gas main. The soldiers were overcome by carbon monoxide fumes in the hole. There was a further delay whilst this was repaired and the soldiers were sent to hospital.

Down and down they went, hour after hour, encouraged by Lieutenant Davies. Occasionally they had to dive for cover as the whistles of the falling bombs from the latest raid came close. An article about the incident from The Daily Mail *noted that 'these gallant – yet most matter of fact men of the Royal Engineers are many a time running a race with death.' By Sunday morning almost 80 hours had elapsed since the bomb had fallen. Then from the pit came a shout: Sapper Wyllie had uncovered the monster's lair, 27 and a half feet down. It was a monster, eight feet long and weighing a ton.*

Two lorries in tandem were needed to winch out the beast. Preceded by police motorcycles, the truck sped through East London until it reached Hackney Marshes. There the bomb was detonated by Lieutenant Davies. The bomb blasted a hole one hundred feet wide and shook plaster from the walls of nearby houses.

Both Lieutenant Davies and Sapper Wyllie were later awarded the George Cross for their actions on this day.

Afterwards, Bob Davies tried to explain to his wife that he wasn't a hero. 'Still the same old dad!' he said.

But the Government and the country needed heroes. John had enjoyed the story as much as everyone else. To find out he was in the company of such men was thrilling.

Sadly the fame he hadn't wanted turned to notoriety for Lieutenant Bob Davies. He was sent to prison for eighteen months in 1942 for theft, taking money he'd been given for saving owners' properties which should have been passed on to the Royal Engineers and handling stolen goods from bombed sites, namely two sets of lingerie, one sent to his wife and one to a lady friend. He later emigrated with his family to Australia and lived in Lakemba, a suburb of Sydney, where he died in the 1970s. I visited Lakemba in the 1970s, too. It's where my uncle and aunt lived and shopped. Another coincidence. Had my uncle or aunt met him? I asked my aunt if she could remember either Bob Davies or his family, but she couldn't.

Bob Davies sold his George Cross. The medal is now owned by a firm of solicitors occupying offices overlooking Dean's Yard, a fitting place for it to end up.

John found out that his job as apprentice architect had signposted him to Bomb Disposal. The training that an architect had in structural engineering, planning and understanding where services were positioned meant they were top of the list and had a head start when dealing with dangerous UXBs and their extraction. His time at Chorley also helped his knowledge of explosives and their volatility.

'All of us got so hooked on bomb disposal: it was such an interesting thing. It was dangerous but it was interesting. It wasn't heroic stuff, but you were doing a recognised job.'

Most of us would disagree. It was surely the most dangerous job with every chance it may result in death or serious injury. And didn't they protect the civilian population and their property and keep up morale?

John described the gratitude shown them by ordinary folk. 'We were cheered and thanked and appreciated for what we were doing and people were well aware of the many heroic acts to save their homes and also the fearful situations bomb disposal units found themselves working in.'

The RE BD Badge

John explained in his notes how the BD men got their special red and gold sewn badge they wore on their jacket sleeves:

'One day early in the war Queen Mary was out in her grounds when a team of BD men walked past. She stopped them and asked who they were, as they had no regimental badge.

They said they had none.

She said she would have it made for them. It was designed

and stitched by her Needlework Guild.'

The original badges were issued as rectangles but always cut into ovals before being sewn onto the left cuff of uniforms.

CHAPTER V
TEN WEEKS AND TICKING

Royal Engineer bomb disposal only began during WWII. The police and Home Guard soon became overwhelmed. The clearance and the disruption caused needed the expertise of the Royal Engineers. In September 1939, it was decided by the War Office that they would provide temporary bomb disposal (BD) teams until the Home Office could recruit and train special Air Raid Wardens to do so. The first teams consisted of an NCO and two sappers, who were required to locate the bombs, dig down and blow them up in situ.

The first bombs to be dropped on the UK were in the Orkneys in October 1939, while the first unexploded bombs (UXBs) fell on the Shetlands in November 1939. The Formation Order of May 1940 formally handed responsibility for bomb disposal to the Royal Engineers and 25 Bomb Disposal sections were formed; soon that increased to 134. Despite almost non-existent equipment and little training, the resourcefulness of the Royal Engineers helped them to learn fast.

In June 1940, just 20 unexploded bombs were dealt with. This rose to 100 in July, 300 in August, and over 3000 by September, so RE BD Companies were increased in number to meet the huge demand. Between September 1940 and July 1941, over 24,000 bombs were made safe and removed.

Those first teams carried a minimal amount of equipment in a truck with 50 bags to fill for sandbags. They were to put the sandbags around the bomb and blow it up where it landed. But that wasn't always the best plan, so that's when the expertise of the first BD officers was used to defuze the bombs before they were taken away to blow up. The fuze was taken out, as once that happened the explosives in the bomb were inert. Sometimes if they couldn't get to the fuze or it was jammed, they removed the explosives from the end of the bomb. Each time they started a new job they were fully aware that it could be their last.

Before the outbreak of war, the Government's chief worry about any attack by the German Luftwaffe was the scale of civilian casualties. It was predicted that 1.8 million people would be killed or wounded in the first six months of enemy bombardment. In fact, the total proved far lower, at 55,000. And at first, the bombs that fell were few and far between and unexploded bombs fewer still. When found, their basic fuzes could be disarmed easily with extractors and dischargers quickly invented for the task.

The job of a bomb disposal officer was still relatively new when John started his training in 1941. When one of his fellow officers asked for some more information, someone at the back called out, 'ten weeks' life expectancy!' There was silence then a nervous laugh or two. That weird sense of wartime humour took over. It seemed to permeate every occasion in the war, often the grimmest, and kept them all going. At the end of the training course, John told his CO that he found that earlier remark very depressing.

'Do you have anything good to tell us, sir?' he'd asked.

'As it happens, I have,' the CO had replied.

'The medical boffins have discovered that bombs explode faster than the human nervous system can react, so don't worry, you won't feel a thing.'

Despite this alarming news, John said that he couldn't wait to lay his hands on his first bomb.

When he got to talk with other officers and they shared experiences, this so-called 'fact' was discussed, and for some it made a difference. Stuart Archer was one of John's hero colleagues. A couple of years older than John, he was already an architect at the beginning of the war and working in South Wales along the coast from John's 16 Company. His heroic deeds were soon the subject of many conversations. Fellow officers marvelled at his amazing courage. He defuzed over 200 UXBs and received the George Cross for gallantry in the face of the enemy. He said that knowing he wouldn't be injured or mutilated but totally blown away gave him more strength and courage. He took chances to dispose of bombs that he might have otherwise hesitated to even touch. He survived like John and lived to celebrate his 100th birthday.

Not everyone agreed with his views, though, or got their strength in that way. And some like John felt it was automatic. 'I just went into auto drive and let things happen. I knew it was dangerous of course – one wrong move and the bomb could easily blow up.'

He also said, 'I think we all discovered in ourselves perhaps attitudes and ideas that we had not realised were there. As soon as I got into bomb disposal I found I had the ability to go into 'autopilot' almost. When faced with a situation I was able to switch everything else off. There was no excitement, no fear, just a methodical drill to tackle a problem. You were always mindful of the fact that you could be there one minute and gone the next, of course. There was a tremendous buzz about it as well. You were very young. You had this tremendous responsibility.'

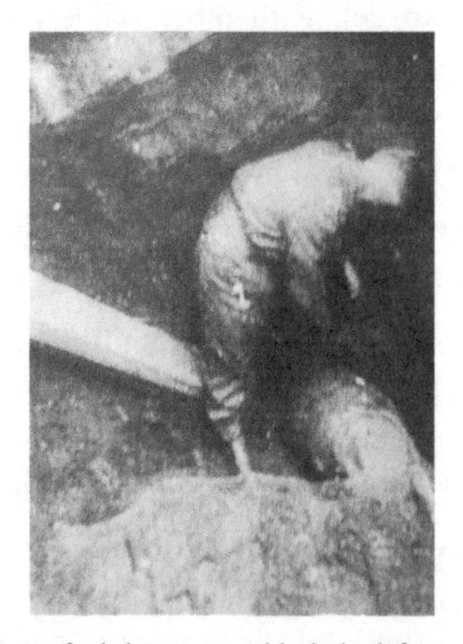

Lieutenant Hannaford down a muddy hole defuzing a large bomb

On a radio programme years later following the documentaries *Danger UXB* for Channel 4, John answered questions from his listeners. One asked: 'The adrenaline flow must have been tremendous when defuzing a bomb. What on earth did you do to return to 'normal' after you successfully completed a job?'

John replied, 'This might sound odd but the flow of adrenaline was the last thing we wanted. When you are dealing with a bomb the last thing you want is adrenaline to flow. You have to be calm and collected and methodical: that was the only chance to get through it. Any adrenaline and you were dead.'

Everyone was keen to point out how luck as well as knowledge was a key factor. Teams and individuals had their lucky charms or set ways of carrying out their dangerous jobs: anything to build confidence at the darkest moment when the fuze ticked away and the seconds stretched your nerves to breaking point.

John said: 'I was a young man about 22 years old and all of a sudden I was given this enormous authority, something I had never had in my life before. The police wanted to know who I was, where I was, how they could contact me, and so on. If a bomb dropped in the middle of Newport the police, would come to me and ask what areas should be evacuated. This was heady stuff for a young fellow. I don't think it went to our heads, but it was part of the deal. You were somebody.'

Most people assumed that bombs would detonate on impact. However, in World War II not all did, either by accident or by design. UXBs came in two forms. Some were bombs whose fuzes had not had enough time to charge in flight, as they had been dropped from too low an altitude. They continued to charge once they had landed, and anything that mimicked the shock of impact, like a blow from a pick or the vibrations set up by a passing truck, might set them off.

The second type of UXB was deliberately designed not to explode when it hit its target, causing major disruption.

From July 1940 the Luftwaffe began sustained attacks on English ports and industrial cities. Initially, a large proportion of high-explosive bombs were used, of which more than 90 per cent exploded on impact, causing civilian casualties and extensive damage. The remainder that did not explode were sometimes faulty or they were fitted with delayed-action fuzes to cause more disruption. Often they penetrated to considerable depths and became lodged close to factories, power installations and other vital buildings, or on airfields and in dockyards. Production came to a halt and everyone in the immediate vicinity had to be evacuated. Roads, railways and other communications central to the war effort ceased to function effectively until the bomb disposal teams had dealt with the bombs. Occasionally even the BD teams were flummoxed. One bomb that got away fell into a moving goods train and travelled up the country before being discovered and disposed of.

Bomb disposal was described as a game of cat and mouse as the British scientists, or boffins, as John called them, tried to outwit Hitler's scientists and learn how to defuze each new type of bomb and so that they could be removed and blown up in a controlled manner to avert the horrific devastation they could cause.

When the first bombs fell on the British mainland in 1940 the Army knew, in John's words, 'sweet damn all' about how to defuze them. As he soon found out during training, they were issued only with primitive tools and had very little besides a metal prod to locate the bombs. You looked at the hole to gauge the size and trajectory of the bomb, then you set the sappers to work digging down, hoping that they'd find it. The tail ripped off as it travelled into the ground, and then it would often change direction.

The sappers worked in shifts. It was a back-breaking job. Then they had to shore up the sides. They had some wood with them, but also used wood from other bombed sites to prevent the huge hole from caving in as they descended deeper to reach the bomb. After many hours and sometimes days they finally would call in the officer to defuze the monster. It was always the officer's responsibility to defuze the bomb with the sergeant close by at the top of the hole. Once the sappers had prepared the site, they moved off to a safe distance. This could take more agonising hours before they used some rope and a pulley system to haul the heavy bomb up using a gyn, to heave it to the surface. Often they had to dig 20 to 30 feet down: the deepest UXB was found under Marble Arch at a depth of 80 feet. There were no machines to help, just the sappers, hand digging with picks and shovels.

Lt Hannaford using a prod to locate a bomb

It was in the Spanish Civil War that an observant German officer realised that an unexploded bomb could cause much greater disruption to the war effort and to civilian morale. So they employed a brilliant German engineer called Herbert Rühlemann to devise a series of anti-handling and delayed-action fuzes. When the Luftwaffe chief Hermann Göring initially showed no interest, the engineer offered his designs to Britain's War Office, where the drawings languished forgotten until after the war. During an interview in his eighties John was asked, 'How did you feel when you found out the UK Patent Office had the information on the fuzes?'

John replied, 'How many rude words do you know? Put them all down! I only found that one out in July 2000 and I couldn't believe what I was being told. Understanding the designs could have saved many lives and also many 'man' hours trying to understand the fuzes in order to remove them.'

Rühlemann visited Britain before WWII broke out. As a guest of the Government he was shown around and visited air shows where he would have seen British designs and been able to make a fair judgement of our capabilities, or lack of them, at the time. The brilliant engineer had made simple mechanical fuzes more versatile by powering them with electricity. This allowed them to control the exact moment of the explosion, which could be delayed by a few seconds or many hours after a missile had hit its target. It made aerial bombing much more effective and deadly. Even if the bomb did not detonate straight away because its mechanism had failed to start, any disturbance days or months later might jog it into deadly readiness. John was to be reminded of this many years later when he discovered a local East Sussex Bomb Disposal team's grave and their tragic story, which happened years after the Battle of Britain.

The Russians failed to headhunt the brilliant scientist so after the war ended Rühlemann emigrated to America and he continued his work as a scientist helping them with their defence programme and later the war in Vietnam. In his autobiography written 40 years after the end of the war, he made no condemnation of the Nazis and, like many, had closed his eyes to the horrors of war. He was proud of his team: 'We were a group of dedicated people working for a common goal. It was our job!'

For more than 2,000 days, Britain was under aerial siege. In total 147,000 British civilians were killed or injured by bombing, the majority during the Blitz and V-weapon attacks. John wrote: 'The sight of RAF pilots flying high and winning the Battle of Britain is quite rightly etched in our memories. However, despite their heroic efforts, bombs continued to fall and many failed to explode.'

Winston Churchill visiting heavily bombed Battersea, South London, 10th September 1940. Courtesy of BBC

Winston Churchill told them that the bombs needed clearing whatever the cost.

Churchill grasped at once the potential threat that these time bombs presented to both the nation's infrastructure and its morale. He fired off an urgent memo to the War Office, ordering that the Royal Engineers Army Bomb Disposal teams and their colleagues in the Navy and the Air Force tackling the same life-threatening but necessary work be given the resources, equipment and recognition needed for their 'highly dangerous work'. And to stop the rivalry and wrangling between services he ordered them to work together, supporting each other and sharing the intelligence they had on each type of bomb. They had to get on with it, regardless of the toll.

John started his bomb disposal training in Cardiff where he shared a room with an experienced officer for six weeks. One night when the officer was out, he heard a ticking sound. A German fuze was on the mantelpiece ticking away. It was a prank. John wasn't surprised as he was classed as a rookie, and in the Army many pranks were played on you if you were a newcomer. At Aldershot he had witnessed the new men being woken in the middle of their first night by officers who made them get up, dress, and then march up and down the road outside the barracks for an hour. Afterwards they told them they were in the Army now and that they had to be up with their new guns cleaned and ready for drill at 8 o'clock. The senior officer in charge couldn't understand (or chose not to) why they were all so exhausted on their first day.

John later discovered that he had replaced Lieutenant Thomas Blackwell in South Wales, who had been relocated to the island of

Malta to support their solitary beleaguered bomb disposal unit. It was under extreme pressure due to virtually continuous bombing by the Italian Regia Aeronautica and German Luftwaffe. Malta is situated close to Sicily at the toe of Italy. The island lay between the enemy to the north, only a few miles away, and to the south beyond the busy Mediterranean Sea, North Africa, where the enemy troops led by Rommel were fighting the war to gain control in the desert over Field Marshal Montgomery and the British Army, the Desert Rats. Malta therefore had a key strategic position in the Mediterranean. Lieutenant Blackwell needed all his training and strength. He survived the war with a distinguished record.

John discovered the connection when author of *Malta UXB*, Susan Hudson, contacted him. Her research had connected John to her father's story. Lieutenant George Carroll served in Malta throughout the war and was an amazing officer. He survived the constant bombardment and lack of resources whilst defuzing UXBs and keeping the population of the island safe.

Malta BD memorial

Many decades later, Prime Minister Joseph Muscat, officially acknowledged their heroic deeds in Upper Barrakka Gardens in the capital city of Valletta. He unveiled a plaque in their honour in September 2017. Cannons fired their booming acknowledgement over the beautiful harbour, which was a fitting tribute to their bravery. Officers past and present from all services honoured the resilience and courage of the Bomb Disposal team on the island fortress. Chairman of the Royal Engineers Bomb Disposal Officers Club Lt. Col. Rod MacArthur, who commanded a Bomb Disposal Squadron for two years, attended the ceremony. With a somewhat astonishing stroke of good fortune my husband and I were on holiday in Malta, too, following John's story. So we were able to attend to watch the unveiling and celebration for those courageous Bomb Disposal officers and men John recognised as heroes. Captain Hannaford would have been so impressed that they were finally receiving deserved recognition, and I'm sure would have hoped the same might happen at home in the UK.

John's training continued as he was sent to Ripon in North Yorkshire for three weeks. The course was intensive and memorable because of a mix-up. Another team exploded a practice bomb and John said, 'But for a good thick hedge his career would have ended then and there.'

On another occasion his good training and knowledge of the BD Manual saved the life of his sergeant whom he stopped from invoking the half-hour rule. The explosion would have killed him and John never forgot his thanks.

John passed his training and was sent to Swansea where he

worked with another experienced officer.

'Well,' he noted, 'six months more experienced in bomb disposal and training than I was.'

The officer was an engineer like his famous father before him. His name was Lieutenant Edward Douglass. John liked him right away. He was older than John and knew Devon well. His father had been a lighthouse engineer and designer for the new Eddystone Lighthouse, the Bishop Rock Lighthouse in the Scilly Isles, and the Fastnet Rock lighthouse in County Cork. He was highly regarded and was a Freeman of the City of London as was Lt. Douglass. Father and son had been in a tragic accident off Dartmouth when their boat had capsized, and they were both thrown into the water. They swam for three-quarters of a mile but his father became increasingly exhausted. Edward tried to keep his father afloat, but sadly he drowned despite his son's best efforts and before a pleasure steamer rescued him. He was only sixteen at the time.

John described him as 'like a father figure'. He respected him and they worked well together. John said, 'It was the best sort of training, as it was one to one.' Shadowing the lieutenant meant he was shown first-hand how to carry out the job. He trained John in the various methods of defuzing bombs, checking the fuze, carefully following the guidance about the latest German fuzes that had been discovered by the scientists at the War Office, and then learning ways necessary to complete the procedure safely. He was well liked and respected in 16 Company.

Swansea was targeted in one of the last bombing raids of the war. In February 1943, Swansea hospital was hit but the bomb failed to go off. The UXB was classed as a category A1, which meant the bomb had to be removed at any cost to the Bomb Disposal squads.

UXBs had different priorities. If they were near hospitals, docks, railways or factories, that would stop the war effort and undermine morale they were classified as A1 by the Regional Commander and were to be dealt with immediately whatever the cost. They went down in grade through B and C, which were priority due to the proximity of civilians, and D if it dropped in a field. It was therefore considered no threat to anyone and could be left until there was time to defuze it.

The hospital in Swansea had to stay open. There had been many casualties. It was perched on a hill and the Civil Defence called to ask their local Royal Engineer BD officer to defuze the unexploded bomb and clear it away as soon as possible to the bomb cemetery on the outskirts of the town. It had been a busy night; it would have been John's call but he had already been sent to London to train US officers. So Lieutenant Douglass attended the UXB at the hospital in his place. John's driver Austin drove the lieutenant there. When they arrived they could see the damage to the side of the hospital wall, and also the crater with the bomb sticking out. It was a coldish morning and Austin asked the lieutenant if he could go to relieve himself before they started. Lieutenant Douglass told him to go behind a nearby wall. It saved his life. Austin headed off and seconds later as the lieutenant went towards the bomb, 'up it went' is how Austin described it to John later.

John described the tragic scene in an interview many years

later as his shocked driver had described it to him. Austin told him how he'd searched around everywhere, but there was nothing left of Lieutenant Douglass. The earth where he'd stood was bagged up, weighed and put in his coffin, then sealed and returned to his family for burial.

John was devastated and the whole of 16 Company shaken. Lieutenant Douglass had been one of the longest-serving and most popular officers. In the section's war diary in the National Archives, the officer on duty reported: 'we have also lost our Lieutenant Douglass who was killed while on Bomb Reconnaissance'. The rest of the diary entries were notes on procedures, ordering of stores and movement of men for training: nothing involving any sentiment so that word 'our' held real emotion. John remarked in a later interview, 'I missed that one.'

He never forgot the lieutenant. John remarked sombrely, 'I can still sharply feel the loss of Lieutenant Douglass,' just like when he'd first been told the news of the horrific accident. The training John received from the lieutenant meant he owed his life to him.

Researching Lt. Douglass's story I was able to find, with the help of the Royal Engineer site and their roll of honour, his headstone along with the Douglass family memorial in St Perox churchyard in Dartmouth. I discovered that his wife Muriel died in 1972 and their only daughter had sadly died at a year old before the war. John thought Edward Douglass had two children. I haven't found them in the research but it would be good to think he has family who might read this account and know of the high esteem in which he was held by John and his fellow officers and men of 16 Company.

John's eyes were wide open when assessing fully a situation before carefully proceeding with each task. It was a good thing, too, in the most testing and dangerous situations. When things were out of his control, his luck remained, which always surprised him and he often questioned it.

Safety was top priority. He was an ideal bomb disposal officer. By nature he was a cautious man, not prone to taking risks, and his pre-defuzing thoughts were as follows: 'I possibly will not survive this but if it happens it will be blissfully quick.'

He now had the knowledge and a useful set of skills. His strength of character and positivity played a huge part, as did his sense of humour, but as time went on he said he was getting increasingly philosophical and moved by the events around him.

As a leader he had been advised to keep his distance and not share his worries with his men, putting into practice his team-building training and at the same time working alongside them and keeping them safe. The enormous pressure on himself as a young man was considerable and would eventually lead to ill health, as it did for many of the BD officers and their men.

Later, John learnt he could have requested a transfer after six months. He said he never knew of this option nor of anyone asking to move.

CHAPTER VI
AN IDEAL CANDIDATE

John was asked in an interview if he volunteered for bomb disposal. He replied, 'Did I bloody hell! I'm not daft.'

John as a young Bomb Disposal Officer

However, John was seen as an ideal candidate for the job and had that curious affinity with bombs.

He'd had that early encounter on the Embankment as his

mother pushed him in the pram. Then working at ROF Chorley already filling and supplying bombs at the outset of war. He knew more than most of the ins and outs of ordnance and the volatility of the chemicals used to fill them, and therefore he was already very safety-conscious because of it. Bombs seemed to follow his family, too. He said his poor parents had to endure a bomb that actually dropped on the village green and bounced over the London Inn at Shaldon on the estuary of the Teign, where they lived and his father was publican. It luckily missed the building by inches. His father said that it had topped all the stories in the bar for many weeks and got his father, a jolly man who enjoyed a tale or two, a few complimentary beers. His mother must have felt very lucky for the second time in her life.

On the Home Front, as the bombing of our cities increased, the workload of those protecting the country became overwhelming, and the spirit of survival took over. The Government were keenly aware of the fragility of the spirit of the civilian population. Protection of all that was held dear was a top priority, as was the morale needed to keep people trying their best amidst so much destruction and upheaval. Keeping the daily business of our nation at war moving was tough but essential.

The bombs that fell on our cities were all part of a strategic plan by the enemy to target the infrastructure, the economy as well as the morale of our citizens. There were also the bombs sent to deny freedom of movement and cause as much disruption as possible. These bombs by design or failure to function would land amongst communities, threatening the safety of all nearby: the UXBs.

Some bombs devastated whole neighbourhoods. Other bombs caused massive fires that raged through homes and factories. There were horrific stories, some not emerging till 70 years later, like the school blast at Canning Town in the East End, which remained unreported until a survivor raised awareness. Only a few who were very young can now recall it. The reports were finally discovered in the National Archives at Kew. At least 600 people were killed in the basement of Hallsville Junior School. They were told to gather at the school to be evacuated. It was close to the docks. They waited three days to be evacuated with bombing happening all around them, and tragically on the fourth day a German bomb split the building in two, exploding in the basement. The building then collapsed in on it. Many of the bodies were never recovered. It was a terrible and devastating time for the community.

Sir James Anderson, the then Home Secretary, reported to Prime Minister Winston Churchill that 'persons in the East End had been made homeless', not mentioning the enormous death toll for fear of damaging further civilian morale. After that dreadful bombing incident, people were allowed to go down and shelter in the Underground stations and sleep there overnight. Guided there by wardens and comforted by volunteers, they waited for the howling sirens and the sound of crashing bombs to stop and fall silent before emerging to carry on with their lives.

During the Blitz there were 76 consecutive days of enemy bombing in London softening us up for a potential invasion, which luckily never materialised. Once the Battle of Britain started, hundreds of unexploded bombs needed defuzing and had to be removed. With growing knowledge, the men of the bomb disposal teams worked tirelessly to find ways of defuzing these first bombs. There were still horrific accidents. It didn't seem to matter how careful you were. There had been cases like that of Captain Max Blaney, as experienced as you could be at that early stage of the war. But by all accounts a careful officer. He was killed along with his whole unit, all of them blown up, even though all the correct procedures had been adhered to. That's why the men believed that luck had a great deal to do with it. Max Blaney and his men died on Friday the 13th.

John was in charge of 35 men of 8 Section, Number 16 Bomb Disposal Company, based at Newport in South Wales. They were 30 miles or so from the main camp, an independent unit and John said he felt quite isolated. It was a great responsibility for such a young officer, which he took very seriously. His unit of men were important to him. He felt they looked after each other. He was known to be careful and didn't take unnecessary risks and luck was with him, though he couldn't fathom why.

He studied the information about the new fuzes, which was sent out daily on the teleprinter, and the men appreciated his cautious approach. John said they were real characters, tough and hard-working, laughing and always making jokes.

He remembered the men well and could still remember their voices right to the end of his life.

He had two staff sergeants and two lance sergeants, backed up by four corporals with two stripes and four lance corporals, including one despatch rider. The rest of the men were sappers whose chief job was to dig down once the officer had located the bomb. They made safe the steep walls of the hole. The tools, the ropes and pulleys to heave the heavy bombs out were all stored in the unit lorry. Once defuzed, the bomb was loaded on the lorry and taken to the bomb cemetery, usually a quarry on the edge of town, to be blown up safely. They had a radio communication line, which was placed inside the bomb hole next to the fuze and connected to the lorry driver. If the fuze started ticking he alerted the sergeant who would shout to get the officer out quickly.

Training Section 8

John's men with Section 8 lorry used to transport bombs

Section 8 had two lorries, both reliable American Ford 3-tonners, which carried their equipment and the team of men to the bomb-site. John now had his own Austin Utility and a batman who drove him to the bomb-sites. He was pleased to again have some fine transport for himself and the unit. They were out in the country and needed the lorries and the car to get around the remote countryside, and deal with the difficult conditions on the roads.

There were more complex and specialised tools as the war progressed and bomb fuzes changed and became more technically sophisticated.

There was little training at first as John found out from so-called 'experienced officers' maybe just a few weeks or, if they'd been lucky, months longer in the job. They'd bravely tackled those first UXBs of the war virtually unaided, literally feeling their way, learning as they completed each job and with luck not getting killed.

The confidence bomb disposal officers had in dealing with such dangerous new weapons depended a great deal on the almost daily technical information and advice provided by the Royal Engineer department known as IF & DBD. Within this department a committee of some 20 leading specialist scientists – John called them 'boffins' – worked together to provide details of the latest German bomb developments and the knowledge to deal with them. They were continually searching for solutions to these new and ever-evolving fuzes. The contraptions they produced often ended up looking like a Heath Robinson design. John described these men as 'brilliant and doing an absolutely amazing job'.

The meticulous engineering of the German technicians also helped the Bomb Disposal teams, as they always numbered their fuzes, and as solutions were found to stop the fuzes, this was the first thing you searched for when uncovering the bombs and opening the fuze pockets. Training was crucial for their survival.

The bombs were charged on the plane, but this process was not complete until the bomb had fallen some distance from the aircraft. If anything went wrong, then the bomb would not go off and became an Unexploded Bomb (UXB). Some bombs were designed to explode immediately. For example, a number 15 fuze was armed to explode on impact, but others were designed to have delays. A number 17 fuze contained a clockwork timer, which created delays of between two and 80 hours. 10% of bombs didn't go off which were troublesome UXBs designed to slow everything down and all to the enemy's advantage.

Rühlemann, the chief German engineer, designed over 60 different fuzes, many of which were meant to kill the officers who tried to defuze them. His number 50 fuze was placed in a pocket, which was ultra-sensitive and would detonate at the slightest touch.

Then there was also the Y fuze, which was charged to last up to two weeks when it left the plane, but included a built-in battery which could help it run for a year. John despaired when he heard this at a training session for officers that he attended at 1 Hyde Park in London in 1942. It seemed the end. Then one of those remarkable scientists he so admired stepped up to instruct them how to defuze it using a plug of Plasticine, the same material children used to play with at school. Then filling it with liquid oxygen, which stunned them all as they watched its icy steam float around the fuze as it was poured in, like magic – hey presto, freezing it and stopping it. Bravo! They all cheered.

By now there were a variety of items used to disarm the fuzes. There was a 'Steven's clockstopper', which had pink liquid that was pumped in under pressure to stop the clock. Then there was a magnetic clockstopper, which had a heavy magnet with a battery, which you turned on, and you heard the clunk as it stopped the clock, and you breathed a sigh of relief. It was a fierce battle of wits, with a high fatality rate every time a new fuze was discovered. There had to be one that failed to blow up. Then it was quickly taken to the scientists to discover its secrets before passing on the valuable information to the BD units.
In John's notes he describes Max, the largest bomb:

'The intriguing story of the German SC 2500 KG bomb, the largest bomb dropped by the Germans during WWII.

We know the first SC 2500 KG bomb was dropped on the UK during the night time 20/21st November 1940 but details of the bomb and its A.Z. 24 A fuze and indeed the bomb itself were not recorded until April 1942. Uniquely Bomb Disposal officers in the field were not informed of this major addition to the German bomb armoury. The few surviving WWII Bomb Disposal personnel were surprised indeed only to learn of the existence of 'Max' 60 years later.

RE Dos and Dont's of Bomb Disposal sketch

The question – why were Bomb Disposal personnel denied this vital information? – now needs an answer. Such confidence BD personnel had in dealing with such dangerous weaponry rested a great deal in the almost daily technical information and advice provided by the Royal Engineer department known as IF & DBD. Within this department a committee of some 20 leading specialist scientists met almost on a daily basis to provide details of the latest German bomb developments and the wherewithal to deal with them.

There are two possible answers why this information was withheld:

1 Of all bombs dropped, of whatever category, roughly 10% failed to explode. For whatever reason no 'Max' bomb failed to do its job: they all exploded. It follows that the technical information found in the 'Restricted' document dated April 1942 must have been acquired through wartime Intelligence sources.

2 It can only be speculation why BD personnel were withheld this information, but there are two possibilities:

1 The IF & DBD committee knew about the bomb, as suggested through Intelligence, but thought it prudent to await an unexploded specimen; the information could then have been based on technical fact.

2 The extraordinary devastation caused by the Max bomb dropped on Hendon, London 13th Feb. 1941 where over 700 houses were demolished or severely damaged and 600

> made homeless may have caused authorities to censor the information to suppress panic among the population. In support of the latter from Britain's perspective, at the time the war prospects were looking very bleak indeed.

The Max bomb sixteen feet long and three feet in diameter had an aluminium casing and was filled with Traileen or a mixture of amatol with RDX and aluminium powder.

Extraordinarily, the Germans having produced this massive bomb found a problem in delivering it to its target. The twin-engined German bombers were not designed to take that size of bomb or its weight. Initially only one Unit was allowed to carry Max and that in specially adapted Heinkel 111s and in that unit only 2 pilots were qualified to fly them.'

John wrote: '70 years on a neighbour, Jean Raabe, during a discussion revealed she and her family lost their house but were not injured in the explosion caused by the Max bomb in Hendon in February 1941. There was extreme devastation and loss of life. An outdoor memorial service was held but the incident was suppressed on national news because of possible widespread panic.'

Below is the range of bombs, which the Germans had at that time:

50kg (112 lb) S.C. or S.D.
250kg (550 lb) S.C. or S.D.
500kg (1000 lb) S.C. or S.D.
1000kg (2400 lb) S.C. (Herman)

1000kg (2400 lb) S.D. (Esau)
1400kg (3200 lb) S.D. (Fritz)
1800kg (4000 lb) S.C. (Satan)
2500kg (6000 lb) MAX

S.C. stood for Spreng Cylindrisch, a thin-walled, general-purpose bomb. The weight ratio of the two types was S.C. 55 percent explosive, whilst the S.D. had 35 percent.

Once the bomb had been located you had to find the fuze to see which number it was. You hoped it was lying face-up, not hidden underneath. If that was the case you had to use a mirror to see it and that was really awkward. All of this was usually taking place in a muddy hole often waterlogged and with noisy pumps chugging along to keep you and the bomb dry whilst you were working. More often than not you were soaked through with water filling your boots. John said feeling this uncomfortable you still had to stay focused and calm and remember every step of your training. One slip-up and it could be your last.

In John's experience there was another category of bombs, the sabotaged bombs that crashed to earth but didn't explode due to being unarmed and without some necessary component. Brave slave labourers working in the German factories taken from concentration camps risked their lives to help the war effort, sending duds! But until they were tackled they were dealt with in just the same time-consuming way as the other UXBs. John defuzed one such bomb and in the casing was just a piece of German newsprint now brown with age. When he discovered its secret it was like a ray of hope, an unexpected gift, and it made him smile. It would have been a very real risk for the saboteur to carry out the act. They would certainly have been shot if discovered.

The German assembly line was described to me by Steve Venus as a meticulous procedure with numbered items in boxes of parts to be used in each bomb. So the offending fuze would have been secreted away somehow under the usually watchful eyes of the guards, distracted for a moment. The saboteur was surely seconds from death. They would never have known how their bomb cheered the British officer who found it, but he felt their courage in fighting back was splendid. He thanked the brave fellow at the assembly line in the German filling factory. He knew it would have been similar in design to ROF Chorley. Bombs were an expensive commodity to be treated with the greatest respect and carefully guarded, so he wished the courageous fellow good luck for future bomb sabotage opportunities and hoped sincerely that they survived.

The precious paper is in John's family collection.

CHAPTER VII
JUST A JOB

John described the term 'bomb disposal' as misleading in respect of what that entailed. Although something like 50,000 German bombs were dealt with, in John's experience far more time was spent on a multitude of dangerous by-products of war, i.e. our own malfunctioning ordnance, Ack-Ack shells, mines and failed practise ordnance of all kinds.

He says two days of his life as a young Bomb Disposal officer can explain it better. Those two days would alter his perception of bomb disposal ever after and stay with him until the end of his days.

8 Section was responsible for the clearance of bombs in an area of 100 square miles around Newport. The responsibility for young Second Lieutenant Hannaford was enormous, but he could not discuss his anxieties with his men. It was not done, he said. And it was very difficult for other people to understand. It was not easy to imagine lying flat on your stomach in muddy water at the bottom of a 30ft shaft, where the sides could cave in at any moment, running your fingers over a cold, sinister-looking, green-grey steel bomb that could send you to eternity.

One day a note was delivered from the War Office that all Army personnel must receive instruction in 'Dealing with Explosives'. John was surprised as he felt they already were experienced as a Bomb Disposal unit.

They assembled in a Victorian schoolroom and were solemnly advised that explosives were dangerous. Lieutenant Walker, their trainer, of the South Wales Borderers, was a veteran of WWI. An engaging man who tried to keep the men's attention and from John's description was of 'a nice man in his forties, who understood the stupidity of the situation and had laid on a little distraction to give them some cheer'.

The lieutenant drove to a territorial training ground close to the estuary of the Severn with John as passenger. The men followed in their truck. The officers became more acquainted and talked of their respective Army duties, the efforts to keep the men's spirits up and to get them decent food, especially over the Christmas period with them missing their families. They shared their dislike of the freezing cold weather in South Wales. John found out Lieutenant Walker was mentioned in despatches for his commitment and brave actions in WWI. He was by all accounts an experienced soldier. When they arrived he produced a crate of Mills grenades and from behind safety mounds they all enjoyed removing the pins, throwing them like cricket balls and listening to the resounding bangs. The men were in fine spirits.

He then produced his ace trick, a new stun grenade to be used in urban warfare to terrify the enemy wherever they were hiding. He threw it and it bounced on the frozen ground. There was no explosion. Perplexed, he decided they should both go to inspect. John was taken aback as he knew only too well that the rules said in such circumstances they must not approach for 30 minutes. Lieutenant Walker was senior in rank so he didn't say anything and had to accompany him. In his words: 'To his extreme discomfort the lieutenant picked up the grenade and started to unscrew the base.'

John's instinct was to run but his men were watching from behind the safety mounds so he stood as firm as he could, shifting uneasily from foot to foot. Having now removed the base, the lieutenant proceeded to tap it on his hand, hoping to remove the fuze. Instinctively John turned and slowly took a step away. The inevitable explosion blew him to the ground and he felt blood from a wound to his head. Gathering himself up, he turned to see the gravely wounded officer. John described how both his arms to the elbows were missing, his eyes were gone and his forehead was missing.

John later recounted that bizarrely and in a clear voice Lieutenant Walker addressed him. He would always remember that voice telling him to give his wife a message, and even in that distressed state he gave John the details of her address in St Pancras, London.

Extreme shock took over and he remembered nothing until he found himself being patched up in hospital.

Lieutenant Walker died a few hours later.

Returning to his headquarters that day, John somehow managed to phone his commanding officer at Cardiff, explaining as best he could and giving him the facts. He was unbelievably unfazed.

'Thanks, Hannaford. Well, you sound alright to me. I take it you can operate in the field – so carry on. Goodbye!'

It seemed a hurried response to John who was left stunned.

He understood for the first time what severe shock was really like. Because of wartime security he was unable to talk about it, certainly not to his men. He had to remain strong for them. They'd also witnessed the dreadful accident. He couldn't just talk to anyone. It wasn't done.

Evening came, dark but moonlit, and John found himself in Newport wandering goodness knows where, but he later remembered returning to base and having to pass a large, dark opening. It turned out to be the stage door of the white stone-built town hall. It terrified him and it was some time before he managed to pass and return to his base where he said he spent a lonely, shattering nightmare of a night.

Early the next day, he was woken by a telephone call from the police. What was thought to be a sabotaged bomb had been found on a Polish tramp steamer in Newport Docks. Would he kindly dispose of it at his soonest convenience? It was later discovered to have been a booby trap put there by the Irish Republican Army, the IRA who were still fighting against the UK to become an independent republic.

John believed what followed probably in a strange way put him back on the rails.

Reporting to the docks he found a Shell 2-gallon petrol tin, painted red, with suspicious wire sticking out of the top. Still being mentally 'out of this world', he said he picked it up, placed it in the back of his utility truck, and drove it to the quarry allocated as the bomb cemetery on the outskirts of the town.

He remembered thinking that he did not recall any mention in his training of this particular kind of problem. There were to be many more such cases, but he pressed on regardless as he was trained to do.

He noted that the entrance to the quarry consisted of a curved lane. Carrying the petrol can, he soon found a flat-topped boulder suitable for rigging the explosives necessary to destroy the unknown but potentially dangerous contents.

It was frosty and bitterly cold and he had to remove his special officer's leather gloves to prepare the demolition charge, and on completion he lit the fuse wire. Retiring at a relaxed pace towards his vehicle he suddenly realised that in his dazed mental state he had left his precious gloves behind. Sprinting back around the corner, he recovered his gloves but was startled out of his wits to see the fuse wire fizzing away a few inches from the charge. He didn't know what the world record was for sprinting a 'curved hundred yards', but he suspected after that he had a fair chance of holding it.

The explosion was thunderous, with flames and towering black smoke.

'Job well done,' he said to himself putting his gloves back on.

He'd had two narrow misses in two days! He was much more careful after that.

The severe shock John experienced would have had a range of symptoms that he was trying to cope with, and which he briefly alluded to when describing his nightmarish walk through the town.

It's possible to sense the confusion he had and the difficulty of concentrating when facing the next job the following morning and forgetting those precious leather gloves. We don't know about his irritability and mood swings; however, his daughters and his neighbours gave me the impression he could be very difficult at times in later years. A conversation with a therapist suggested there could have been a feeling of guilt, even shame or self-blame. He lost consciousness and felt disconnected. He was certainly numbed by the blast from the stun grenade and he still had the pain from the physical injury to his head to be endured with probably an almighty headache.

In normal circumstances and with time to work through the trauma, the healing process of getting enough sleep, learning to relax again and being able to concentrate with a clear mind would have taken some time. That was probably extremely difficult in the circumstances. His own men must have suffered from watching the accident happen, and he had of course to consider them, too.

It takes varying times to recover from any trauma, from a few days to a few months, often experiencing flashbacks and going over painful memories. John never forgot or coped fully with the loss of Lieutenant Walker, and right up until the month of his death was retelling the sad story of the friendly officer who forgot his training and underestimated the power of the newly designed stun grenade. Steve Venus, John's friend and avid WWII collector, thought it must have been faulty. It was a prototype and it wasn't supposed to maim people, just scare them. Years later, during one of their lengthy phone calls, John told Steve he thought he'd had a breakdown.

It was a terrible burden for a young man to bear, and for so long. Even at the customary inquest John was not allowed to tell the full account, as it was such a sensitive subject. Lt. Walker was described as an expert in his special line. A verdict was given as death by misadventure and recorded by the Coroner. He stated that the loss could have been avoided. The deceased had been overconfident.

John was not able to give the officer's wife the message, which preyed on his mind always. He asked various friends and family to find the address and the officer's family. The address 73 Leighton Road no longer existed, whether after bombing raids or redevelopment. John only discovered where Lieutenant Walker was put to rest in the military section of St Pancras Cemetery when Steve Venus did some research for him. His daughter Jill drove him to look for it. He wanted to go and find it on his own.

After setting off with the same map of where to locate the grave, and with my daughter's help, we discovered the crucial information that St Pancras Cemetery had been moved to East Finchley sometime after the war. When we arrived we were given the directions and we followed it as John had done several years before.

Lieutenant Keith Jerome Jocelyn Walker MBE was in Section 15 RC, grave number 341. After 20 minutes' walk we located the address. We took another 20 minutes or so to locate the discoloured headstone hidden under a tree covered in brambles. It would have been impossible for an elderly John to clamber over the weeds and locate the memorial stone. And it needed two of us to find it. Then it was so discoloured it was camouflaged and forgotten and very hard to read. Jill said he returned to her car saying he was unable to find it and somewhat disgruntled.

It was a wonderful feeling finally discovering Lieutenant Walker for John. We left flowers and a message about how John had never forgotten him. With the support of the Royal Engineers we were able to contact the Commonwealth War Graves Commission and have his headstone, which had been placed there in 1942, returned to its pristine state befitting the brave and noble officer who served in two wars.

John's notes repeat the tragic event over many years. It was always clear in his memory but it was only in a later interview that he said the actual words the lieutenant had said to him. He hadn't written them in his earlier notes, only saying that the lieutenant's voice and message were clear despite his horrific injuries. The interviewer described John as being very upset as he told him that he'd said, 'Tell my wife I love her.' Unfortunately, John never got the chance to pass on the message.

No wonder John said the memory of those two days changed his life forever.

LT Walker's headstone

A few months later in early 1942 whilst John was still serving as Section Commander based at Llanishen, Cardiff, a report from the Commanding Officer Major Windle sent him on a 'recce' to Usk. Arriving there, he met the farmer whom he remembered 'as a miserable old bugger': he just wanted to get on with the job and clear out of there as quickly as possible.

They found that a stick of bombs, the collective noun for bombs, had been aimed at the bridge over the River Usk, missed their target and had fallen into an adjoining field, the farmer's field. Most had exploded, one was easily identifiable as a UXB and there was clear evidence that another UXB had landed in the river shallows. All efforts failed to locate that bomb, so John presumed that it still lies there today.

When excavation started on the first UXB the tail of a German 250kg bomb was soon located, and at about fifteen feet the body of the bomb proper was found embedded in gravel.

There was much seeping water and as the River Usk is tidal, only work at low tide was possible. Despite efforts to catch low water, two pumps, an Evans double-diaphragm and an air compressor pump, were barely able to stem the flow. High tide water was being retained by the gravel and continuously released back into the shaft.

Upon exposure, the No. 17 time delay clockwork fuze was found to be undamaged and, as luck would have it, 'sunny side up', as John described it. Despite the two pumps working to capacity it was not possible to fit and operate the 'clockstopper', but he took care to establish that the fuze clock was not ticking. After considering the options and because of the continual ingress of water, it was decided that a fairly quick technique was required.

He remembered how his heart was beating fit to burst. Sweat was streaming into his eyes and his clothes clung to him. He was cold and soaked through and his boots full of muddy water, but he ignored the unpleasant feeling to focus on the job.

He knew the instructions by heart and proceeded to disconnect the complex wiring system. This consisted of fitting a Merrylees extractor to the fuze head and removing the fuze from a safe distance by remote control. Unfortunately at the last pull of the cord and turn of the Merrylees wheel, it jammed and refused to free itself.

At this point and with hindsight, John felt his common sense and training had failed him, as down the shaft he went to investigate the trouble. It was also a question of pride he later said and told an interviewer, "Everyone else had one," but they had been given strict instructions not to remove a 17 by hand and he was about to do just that. Noting that the fuze was almost clear of the pocket, he judged that if a booby trap or ZUS-40 (an anti-handling device designed to make the bomb explode if the fuze was removed) had been fitted, then the bomb would have already exploded. Having removed the extractor, he gently started to ease out the fuze, but what followed was forever in his thoughts and shook him to the very core.

One moment he was ankle-deep in water at the bottom of a shaft echoing to the din of two noisy pumps and in his hand a live, shiny aluminium bomb fuze, then in a split second his small world vanished together with the noise. There was silence. He could see nothing, not even his hands, feet or the bomb. Silence. He vividly recalled thinking it was a peaceful end. He was in Heaven. He waited to see angels appearing through the clouds. A lifetime seemed to pass in seconds, and then from above he heard the reassuring Lancashire voice of his sergeant: 'Are you alright, sir?'

He couldn't remember the exact words of his reply but he thought it might have been a bit rude.

It must have been a ghostly white face that looked up as the clouds parted. The sergeant's face had drained of all colour, too, as he strained to see down into the misty hole.

The explanation rapidly emerged. The rubber hose to the compressor pump had blown off virtually under his feet, thereby vaporising the water into a thick mist. The sergeant, some distance away, seeing what he thought was smoke issuing from the shaft, with commendable presence of mind immediately stopped both pumps and silence followed.

Regaining some sort of composure, he realised that there was one small but vital step, and a life-saving one at that to be made to the fuze. The bomb itself was defuzed, but the clock fuze in his hand still had the all too sensitive gaine attached, which was a combination detonator booster. According to the book, as John had been trained to do, this was rapidly unscrewed and placed safely in his pocket. Making his way up the ladder, fuze in hand, there was a loud, pistol-like crack and what seemed like a sheet of flame shot across his face. The fuze had fired, fortunately when removed from the bomb.

It could have been set to go off anytime in 96 hours, but he got it out with just seconds to spare.

As in all similar cases there was a technical inquest by the scientists in Whitehall, and there was little doubt that through a manufacturing fault the trip mechanism was held back by a rough spot a few ticks from explosion. This meant that if the bomb fuze face had been damaged or hidden and an attempt made to turn the bomb, there would have been casualties. It was yet another close shave.

Following defuzing, the bomb was lifted, placed on a lorry and taken to the bomb cemetery at the old quarry in Newport. There the explosive was steamed out and another incident avoided.

The heavy fuze cylinder, which can fill the palm of your hand, is cracked and blackened. John kept it on his desk, as his treasured memento, for many years. He then passed it to friend Steve Venus to add to his collection, where it remained for another few years. Steve had promised he would give it to John's grandson Dominic, when John died, which he did at the funeral.

Seconds from death, that cold lump of metal could have been the end of John. Instead, it filled John with pride when he looked at it, stirring his memory, linking him to his dangerous past life and reminding him of his good fortune and his lucky escape.

There were lighter moments. Humour was a great healer. When John was based at Narberth in Pembrokeshire he was requested to go and defuze and get rid of a bomb near the village of Rhandirmwyn or, as John jokingly translated, Randy Mowen.

It was going to be tricky to get up to the sheep farm owned by Mrs Jones, as it was high in the mountains and isolated. There was only a farm track to take the American Ford 3-tonner, which would be loaded up with his men and their equipment. He was instructed that a policeman would meet them to open up a gate and give them some directions.

It was indeed very tricky to say the least. There was a sheer drop on the left side, so they drove carefully through the gate and were warned by the policeman to keep to the right and that Mrs Jones was expecting them.

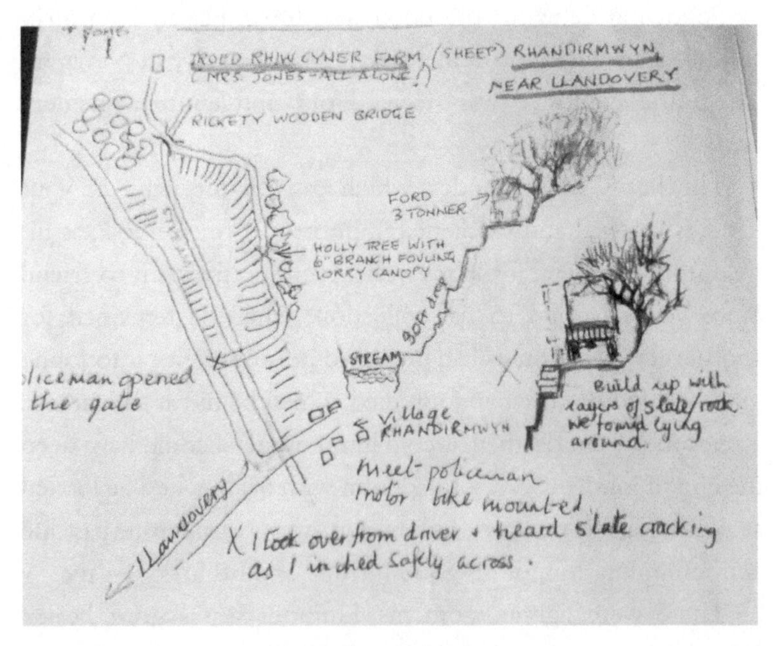

Holly tree sketch

All went well, if a little slowly, until round a bend and up further and higher on the steeply twisting track John and his men spotted an overhanging holly tree. It was on the right-hand side, a prickly problem if ever there was one, as on the left-hand side the track was crumbling away. John's driver tried to creep forward, but he was out of luck this time. The holly branch fouled them. The men in the back ducked as it ripped through the canopy of the truck. They all carefully got out to assess the problem.

They could see the track shelving away but some large sheets of slate were sticking out further along. They were able to use them to lodge them under the left front wheel so they could move on. They cut back the offending branch. John decided to drive and drove forward 'incredibly slowly', as the men looked on. He described to his daughter Jill many years later how 'the patched-up track creaked and creaked as he edged the lorry over it'. Although John enjoyed driving the 3-tonner, that had been a trial even for him. Luckily there were no more mishaps until they had to move cautiously across the rickety bridge below the farm. At last they arrived at Mrs Jones's sheep farm. Her farmhand stood there with his mouth open as they unloaded their equipment. Then he took them over to the field where the bomb had dropped. Mrs Jones was glad to see them and invited John into the farmhouse for a spot of lunch whilst the sappers and his sergeant set about exposing the bomb so that John could defuze it.

'It was a nice perk of the job as the officer in charge.' John thoroughly enjoyed the special treatment.

When he was finally called to the bomb he was surprised to see it was one of our own RAF bombs that must have been jettisoned so the plane could land back safely at base. It was still a surprise and remained a bit of a mystery. One thing was good, though: he knew how to defuze our bombs. He had been trained for that and there would be no booby trap, which sometimes happened with the German bombs. And with this bomb they were sure to be back at the barracks sooner.

It was a straightforward job and they loaded the bomb onto the back of the truck so that it could be taken back to be detonated. They waved farewell to Mrs Jones and her still awestruck farmhand. They were keen to get going as it was getting gloomy and the light was fading. As they went through the nearby village, not even a pin prick of light showed because of the blackout. They slowly manoeuvred through the streets and came to a square and then stopped. It had three roads leading away from it. There were no signs, of course, as they'd all been removed in case of invasion. What were they to do? They didn't want to end up back in the mountains and travelling back along that treacherous track in the dark.

The situation was soon decided for them. There were cheery Welsh voices coming from across the square. They gathered it must be closing time at the local pub. A chink of light appeared as men tumbled out of the place. They came over and John asked for directions. There was more chatting in Welsh and John surmised it wasn't all about sending them in the direction they wanted. In fact, he was pretty sure they were trying to get themselves a lift home on the back of the lorry.

John knew exactly what to do. He took the Welshmen round the back of the truck and lifted the flap up. Even though it was dark, they could just make out the huge bomb resting there. They muttered something that John was glad he couldn't understand, pointed to the road they had to take, and were off like a shot.

He and his men had a good laugh. They got back on the lorry and on the right road. It had been a good day in Bomb Disposal and they were looking forward to a good night's kip.

There was another heart-warming time that John remembered well. He and his team were called out to clear a number of bombs that had narrowly missed a mining village.

He doesn't say where and my research hasn't found out where either, but the bombs had landed in a field close by, too close and too dangerous for everyone to stay there. The whole village might be flattened if the bombs exploded, so he advised that every house be evacuated.

There was a lot of upheaval as families and elderly folk were helped along and young children were either carried or pushed in their prams. There was a long line of carts and wheelbarrows filled with as many belongings as they could pack quickly. They dashed away along the street to the safety zone, with the police and air raid wardens hurrying them and guiding them as they went. When they were all at a safe distance, the BD team were able to start neutralising the UXBs. It took some hours before they could all be safely defuzed then removed.

When the all-clear was given every man, woman and child lined the streets to cheer John and his men. The men felt quite emotional: it was a tear-jerker, John said. They were given presents, anything that was available; cigarettes were popular, as they were hard to get and nearly everyone smoked in those days, including John. They got cakes and even money pressed into their hands which they had to declare. The villagers were so grateful. 'It made you feel elated and very proud to do the job of Bomb Disposal,' John later said. 'You felt like heroes then.'

CHAPTER VIII
COMMANDING OFFICER, 8 SECTION, 16 COMPANY

John had several photos of his 8 Section men. Some were training photos of the men learning knots, dated summer 1942 at Rhoose, South Wales. Knots were an important skill when you were hauling massive bombs out of deep holes. Another has his corporal and a sapper posing and looking very relaxed, considering it says, 'Removing bomb load' with their trusty American truck which took them all over the hilly and difficult roads of South Wales, as well as transporting bombs to the bomb cemeteries to be blown up.

My favourite when I found it was the large group photo below, with probably only a third of the entire section. It looked a good-humoured group with a friendly dog taking centre stage as mascot.

They were John's men and he was proud of them. I turned it over to find out if he had dated it. The message on the back caught me unawares and I was shocked.

Turning back to look once more at those young men, I studied them, looking for answers. How had they died, and when and where exactly? How did John find out?

The writing in 1942 is written in pen. Sadly there are no names. The message about their deaths is written in pencil and was added later.

I found some names from searching through John's notes and on the back of other photos. I hope a relative might read this and recognise a name or a face.

Sgt. Lissemore, B Warmsley, Sgt. Ernest Cant, aged 35, Corporal Ronald Pacey, Sapper Frederick Tennison, aged 24, the same age as John. Could these soldiers be here? There was another just named 'Buckley' and a photo of him deep in a bomb hole and John mentions Lt. Healey. Was he the lieutenant who took over when John left? Probably he was. They may be in this photograph or maybe not.

Section 8 with dog mascot

Local historian Steven John found me the grave and memorial stone for Frederick William Francis Tennison who was killed by a bomb explosion whilst on duty on Easter Monday 26th April 1943. Not at Saundersfoot, but probably further along the coast between Tenby and Penally, as their deaths were recorded at Haverfordwest. If they had died at Saundersfoot they would have been registered in Narberth. I then discovered Sergeant Ernest Cant and Corporal Ronald Pacey, killed by the same explosion on the same Monday.

No 16 Bomb Disposal Company (8 SECTION HQ –
Mt. St. Albans, (CHRISTCHURCH)
Newport. S. Wales. 1942.

nearly all were killed 12 months later
on 'beach' mine clearing Saundersfoot/
Tenby area, Pembrokeshire

J. Hannaford

Message on the back of photo

There was no mention of this in John's notes that had been handed over by his family. However, when he tells the story during his IWM interview he describes how a group of his men were sitting on a sandbank having their lunch and smoking cigarettes after their stint clearing mines on the beach. The next group had started their shift. The mines had been laid at the beginning of the war when there was a strong possibility the enemy would invade. Storms had banked the mines up against each other on the sandy beach and the salty sea air had corroded the fuzes, so removing them was an even more dangerous job. Tragically, John says one blew up across the beach, setting off a chain reaction with explosions ripping across the sands and killing the group up on the sandbank.

It must have been the three soldiers. John said 'nearly all', so more than the three I've found. What could have happened to the other nine in the photograph?

John said he was devastated when he heard the news. He was already in London. Who gave him the news? How did he know it was in the Saundersfoot/Tenby area?

When I looked online for information I automatically looked at Saundersfoot. I needed to check Tenby, too! *The Tenby Observer* wrote an article helping with the search and I still hope there will be more information surfacing one day.

Section 8 posing with young boy

They also have this photo, another great photo of 8 Section men. On the back it says 'Chepstow', which is nearer the Wye Valley in Monmouthshire where John worked as a corporal on his motorbike doing reconnaissance earlier in his training. The Chepstow Beacon also informed its readers and have asked for help. Maybe that young lad, now in his eighties, still lives nearby. He must have been so proud to have his photo taken with the brave BD men.

I tried to find out more by sending posters to the library in Saundersfoot and also to a couple of their care homes where elderly folk might remember some past event, and I searched the Internet for local people who might help. I found a local lady called Penny on their Facebook page. I could tell she was proud of the village, their heritage and history. We had a conversation on the phone. I wasn't sure people there would want to find out about deaths on their beautiful beach, but Penny reassured me and was enthusiastic about finding out about their past and knew others would be, too. Penny said there was a History Society exhibition in August we might learn more there. My husband and I planned our trip right away. She also suggested several other contacts. There was a retired officer at Chapel Bay Fort, an ammunition museum at Angle who might help and Penny put me in touch with Steven John, the South Wales historian who discovered Frederick Tennison for me.

She also suggested I ask the members of a shared Facebook site of 'bygone Saundersfoot and Tenby'. I had a comment back almost immediately from a member and a resident of Saundersfoot telling me of a sighting of three bodies in a tunnel along from their beach which had been spotted when the elderly gentleman was a child in the war. What a result. It seemed to be the answer. I hoped it was.

But Steven John said it was more likely the bodies were of three crew members from a German plane shot down in the bay. There was no record of Bomb Disposal men killed on Saundersfoot beach, he wrote.

When we arrived in Saundersfoot we were given a warm welcome. We met Penny at the beach. It was a beautiful morning and it was already busy with tourists. Penny gave us a guided tour. It had been an important area in 1943 and its seclusion was ideal for an important place to practise for the D-Day landings. The beaches are similar to Normandy and the shallow waters and wide Carmarthen Bay were perfect for Operation Jantzen. The locals were sworn to secrecy and banned from the beach areas. There was a curfew.

The History Society in the little seaside town was particularly helpful. Their exhibition was interesting and well attended. I began to discover more. There was a feast of stories and titbits of information but no further evidence of 8 Section men dying on Saundersfoot beach, although Peter, a local man who grew up in the village, told me he had heard an explosion as a child. Could it have been the mine accident? We chatted about the manoeuvres. There would have been a lot of noise. There were 100,000 troops involved in the exercise, Canadian and other Commonwealth soldiers, the US Army and our own British soldiers. The huge number of troops literally invaded the area, which swarmed with beached supply ships and barges, landing craft, amphibious vehicles, Jeeps, guns, barrage balloons and all the other paraphernalia of a seaborne invasion. Prophetically, as it turned out, the weather was rough, as it was for the real thing, and there were many mishaps involving piled-up barges and landing craft, submerged equipment and resulting explosions.

Peter, a retired headteacher, also had had an adventure that could have gone scarily wrong. He had been involved in the retrieval of a wartime bomb from Saundersfoot beach. He and his friend John had been playing on the beach as children and spotted some metal sticking out of the sand. They dug down and unearthed a bomb. Quickly the local policeman was sent for. He promptly arrived with a wheelbarrow. Peter laughed, as we all did, marvelling at the policeman's solution to the problem. We shook our heads as he continued to tell us how he watched the policeman place the bomb in the wheelbarrow, which he then pushed round to the harbour, over some bumpy cobbles. Peter said he then transferred it to a small rowing boat and rowed out to deep water and dropped it over the side.

What a tale! What about health and safety? we all said. We agreed it could have ended so differently for the two boys and the brave and foolhardy policeman.

It happens that the deaths of the three of 8 Section men were registered at Haverfordwest on the same day as a dreadful loss of life that Easter Sunday weekend at Freshwater West, a bay on the south coast in Pembrokeshire along from Tenby. Possibly they were overlooked because of the awful disaster. Maybe that's what John meant when he said 'forgotten'.

79 men died when two World War II ships sank off the coast.

The British landing craft went down near Freshwater West after getting into difficulty in a storm while travelling from Belfast to Cornwall.

Only three people survived the disaster and many bodies were never recovered.

The landing craft – which were used to deliver troops, equipment and supplies – were on a test journey to see how seaworthy they were when they hit bad weather. They had initially left Belfast for Falmouth, and after briefly docking in Holyhead the weather conditions rapidly deteriorated. For reasons unknown the vessels were denied permission to enter harbours in Fishguard and Milford Haven. The open-decked ships continued in the storm until they reached Freshwater West, but by this point they were in serious difficulty.

The local lifeboat at Angle was undergoing repair at the time and the lifeboat men were left without a means of rescuing the men from the ships.

In a further tragedy, six crew members from HMS *Rosemary*, who also tried to help, died as their rescue vessel was engulfed by a huge wave. The wrecks of the ships remain on the seabed off the Pembrokeshire coast.

On our visit to South Wales I also discovered that ten of 16 BD Company had been killed at Pembroke Dock in April 1942. It was the same year as the date on the back of the photo. But John's comment suggests all his men died on beach mine clearance the year later.

John didn't write about the loss in his notes, only that the numbers of BD men killed were forgotten in history, so not recorded? Where were the others killed by mines?

Newport, where he was based, to Pembroke Dock was 106 miles away, so they were probably men from another Section of 16 Company. He and his Section 8 men were always aware that whole teams could be blown up. Eighteen men were killed instantly on the morning of 28 April 1942 at the Defensible Barracks overlooking Pembroke Dock. Another died the following day after their training course went wrong.

A group of soldiers with the Pioneer Corps were undergoing instruction in the disposal of landmines at the old fort. Steve Venus, John's friend, suspects they were probably defuzing a giant sea mine. Despite Pembroke Dock being very heavily bombed during World War Two, it was the single largest loss of life in the town. There was very little reported at the time because of the wartime censor.

The men are buried at the Llanion Military Cemetery in the town: ten RE Company 16 BD men, three German Jewish refugees who'd escaped from Germany and joined up, and five from a Scottish regiment.

We took Penny's advice and headed on to Chapel Bay Fort, the Ammunition Museum, which was well hidden at the end of the Pembrokeshire Peninsula. It has a rich history and excellent guides and very interesting displays. It was built in 1817 into the side of the hill to protect against a possible French invasion. As you drive on ever narrower roads meeting huge tractors and breathing in as they pass, you can't believe there is any building there to find. What a treasure you discover. It was good to finally see the array of fuzes John had described so precisely and a wide selection of bombs and ordnance he so often described in his notes. It was also great to see Ack-Ack guns and imagine John's description of the ones at New Brighton. He said they'd been peeled back like bananas after the continuous firing on the first night of the sustained bombing of Liverpool Docks. I was delighted when the retired officer knew of John Hannaford and his heroic story. It was so good to hear. How could John believe they were forgotten when at the most westerly point in Wales he was remembered so quickly when I mentioned his name?

After visiting the Ammunition Museum we returned to Saundersfoot once more to search for any hints or explanations to our unanswered questions.

Saundersfoot Beach

We walked along the coastal path, curving round beside the sandy beaches through the small tunnels to Wiseman's Bridge. The tunnels were constructed to allow for the fast transportation of anthracite.

Around the time of the Battle of Trafalgar the best-quality anthracite was being loaded from carts onto beached sailing ketches on the Pembrokeshire coast to be shipped to small ports all round South Wales and the Bristol Channel area.

Clean, smokeless and efficient, it was well known and in great demand in cities like Bristol and Bath, Swansea and Cardiff, and the coal mines across the coalfield from Saundersfoot to St Brides Bay were working feverishly to meet the market. Queen Victoria herself would have nothing else to power her royal ship.

One beach, which was as busy as any, was Wiseman's Bridge, for there were innumerable small pits fairly close to the shore around this coast, and the coal measures extended under the sea in Carmarthen Bay. Wiseman's Bridge lies midway between Monkstone Point and Telpyn Point in the broad, curved sweep of Saundersfoot Bay. The coal industry has long gone, but there are legacies to remind people of it. The tunnels through which the coal trams rumbled to the beach, drawn by the little locomotives of what was jokingly known as the 'Miners' Express', are now shortcuts for holidaymakers and locals between Saundersfoot and Wiseman's Bridge and the same tunnels where a young lad saw some bodies.

Saundersfoot tunnel

It is reported, though also disputed, that Wiseman's Bridge Inn can claim the distinction of having been visited by Winston Churchill in 1943, when he came down with other top war leaders, Lord Louis Mountbatten and General Eisenhower, to watch Operation Jantzen and the spectacular rehearsals for the Normandy Invasion which were played out on the wide expanse of the local beaches between Saundersfoot and Pendine.

Penny had also heard the story but said it was unlikely and that they'd heard that a double was employed by the Government to protect the Prime Minister and keep his whereabouts secret. However, the son of the innkeeper reported that his father saw

Winston Churchill along with his daughter Sarah Churchill, a blonde-haired women in uniform. She was in the Women's Auxiliary Air Force and worked on photographic reconnaissance, interpreting photographs for invasion. I studied the many aerial photographs of Operation Jantzen at the National Archives and wondered if they were the same ones she studied. Her opinion was valued. She was described as a 'quick and versatile interpreter' and she had already helped with Operation Torch, the 1942 invasion of North Africa.

We walked back through the tunnels remembering the memories of a local boy. In the chilly tunnel I had an uneasy feeling and hurried on to the welcoming sunlight. Had John's men walked through them to reach the beach mines?

CHAPTER IX
TEACHING U.S. BOMB DISPOSALEERS, AN ULCER AND THE DESK JOB

John said, 'At the beginning I had immense confidence, but the more I did, the more nervous I got. After two years in Bomb Disposal, I was posted to London to instruct American officers, and it was only then that the effect of the stress became apparent.'

He was relocated to the Duke of York barracks in Chelsea, where the Saatchi Gallery is located today. The United States knew the UK had been under heavy bombardment in the Blitz and 'the Brits knew a lot more than them about defuzing bombs'. Their officers were sent to London to learn as quickly as possible about the disposing of bombs and ordnance. John was one of the officers sent to train them. Several people had commented on his clear descriptions of the workings of bombs. As I listened to him, I could hear for myself from his interviews for Channel 4 and the Imperial War Museum that even at 95 his memories of the intricate operations needed to remove fuzes were accurate and precise.

He was told he was being given an important job and was

promoted to captain to train the Disposaleers as they called themselves. They could only receive training from someone of equal rank or above. It altered the course of John's wartime. It was exciting being promoted and back in London. It brought opportunities to socialise that he'd missed, being in the remote area around Narberth in South Wales.

He didn't know it at the time, but he wouldn't return to Wales during the war or go back to his Bomb Disposal Company.

He was now classed as very experienced in disposing of UXBs and other ordnance. This was his chance to demonstrate that knowledge and pass it on, and also a chance to share his stories with like-minded soldiers.

It was well known that as a close ally to the UK, the US had given support with a trade deal for food and provisions and munitions before the outbreak of war in 1939, and through the first campaigns, which helped ramp up the huge war resources needed. Even with the new ordnance factories where John had worked there weren't enough bombs being produced. So convoys of ships made the dangerous voyage across the Atlantic, avoiding the German Navy and their U-boats as war intensified. The President and Congress still remembered the loss of thousands of their young men so far from home in WWI, and the country was reluctant to repeat that. Though aiding their allies, they wouldn't fully commit and had remained neutral but had imposed restrictions on Germany and Japan.

That all changed at the end of 1941. Just before 8 a.m. on December 7, hundreds of Japanese fighter planes attacked the American naval base at Pearl Harbor near Honolulu on the island of Hawaii. The Americans were totally unprepared for the unexpected attack. The barrage lasted just two hours, but it was devastating. The Japanese managed to destroy nearly 20 American naval vessels, including eight enormous battleships, and more than 300 aeroplanes. 2,000 Americans soldiers and sailors died in the attack, and another 1,000 were wounded. The day after the assault, President Franklin D Roosevelt asked the American Congress to declare war on Japan. They agreed. Three days later, Japan's allies, Germany and Italy, also declared war on the United States; Congress reciprocated. More than two years into the conflict, America had finally joined World War II and they were determined to catch up quickly.

The US Army was a popular diversion in our war-ravaged country. However, they were taking no chances and were carefully briefed on how to behave here. Each was issued with an introductory manual called 'A short guide to Great Britain', produced by the US Army and Navy Departments. 'Never criticise the King or Queen' was one piece of advice, and 'Never criticise the food, beer or cigarettes' was another. The manual also had a glossary at the back to try to prevent misunderstandings. Generally the troops were welcomed. Britain felt they needed all the help they could get. It was reported that the US soldiers were good-natured, generous and friendly. With many British men serving overseas, young women were particularly taken with the new arrivals – no wonder, as they brought everything from money, nylon stockings, cigarettes, sweets and chocolate along with glamour, boldness and Jeeps. John was very interested in their Jeeps.

US officers sent to learn about bomb disposal were under pressure to learn the different methods as fast as they could. John was amazed by their confidence and all the extra rations they had. A common joke was that the yanks were 'overpaid, oversexed, overfed and over here'. John found them amiable enough and certainly keen to learn.

They surprised him on the first day they arrived, not in the Jeeps as he expected, which was a disappointment to him, but in a fleet of taxis all queuing up in a long line outside the barracks and onto the Kings Road. It was quite a sight to behold. It seemed a great extravagance to John who was used to a strictly rationed lifestyle. They marched in across the cobblestones and unfortunately their boots made the most unusual sound, the sound of breaking wind. They had rubber-soled boots and John said it was absolutely hilarious and caused quite an uproar with the waiting Army officers and staff preparing to meet them, so much so that General Alan Brooke, who had an office in the building and was Chief of the Imperial General Staff and Head of the Army and a key advisor to Winston Churchill, appeared and asked what on earth all the commotion was about? John had to tell him. He was not amused and told them in no uncertain terms to get a move on and start the training as planned with no more raucous behaviour. The US officers were to be treated with the utmost respect. Pressure was on and expectations high that they could deliver and get the Allied soldiers up to scratch ASAP.

Training was more organised for the US officers than ever John could remember his had been. Then they'd known next to nothing and been ill-prepared. So many of those first officers and teams lost their lives and the training for the next teams was what not to do. John told the US officers of the risks and the heroic acts of bravery by officers who knew every bomb could be their last. He told those early stories of narrow escapes, his own included when he thought he'd died and gone to Heaven, but managed to get his precious 17. He proudly showed them explaining each step of the operation.

His curved mile record made them roar with laughter, though he didn't explain all the previous days' tragic events; however, he got his safety message across and his methodical approach to defuzing bombs. He made them laugh, but they said it also gave them nightmares. John enjoyed the storytelling and the reactions. It was important work but enjoyable and often proved entertaining.

Unfortunately his training job didn't last long and was cut short when he was struck down with terrible stomach pains. 'I was diagnosed with an ulcer,' he said.

The doctor sent him immediately to hospital to have an emergency operation. John's condition was serious and an operation that could have proved fatal in those days. It was considered major surgery. John was really upset and couldn't believe it when they told him he had a duodenal ulcer. He needed several weeks in hospital and then several more back at home recuperating.

It was the end of his time with the Disposaleers and there was no return to 16 Company in South Wales either, which was even more devastating for John. He knew his unit were being prepared for landing in Normandy, but before that he was told they had been sent to the Saundersfoot and Tenby beaches to clear mines.

Winston Churchill had insisted that thousands of mines should be laid when there had been the threat of the German Army invading. Now they had to be cleared to allow our soldiers safe access to the beaches for the big initiative. In the meantime, there had been some tragic fatalities with the public and stories of children and dogs who'd strayed onto the beaches being maimed or killed.

It was to prove a difficult job. The mines were designed to hold back the invading troops and blow up tanks, vehicles and heavy artillery landing on our beaches, but they had been moved, weathered and had deteriorated, so becoming unstable and hard to find.

John never got over the feeling of guilt leaving his men and then hearing that half of them were killed doing that job.

After his convalescence in Shaldon, he was told to report to Whitehall and given a desk job working for, in John's words, 'the top brass', two Royal Engineer generals for the remainder of the war. He never met the elderly general he'd travelled on the train to Chester with. He would have enjoyed working for him!

His mother bade him a cheery farewell and return to work for a change. That was a first! He'd overheard her talking to a friend about how worried she'd been whilst he worked in Bomb Disposal and how pleased she was that he was out of it.

John returned to London somewhat deflated. There seemed no opportunity for adventure for a young man sitting behind a desk for the rest of the war. Captain John Hannaford had survived daily life-threatening situations and was encouraged to be independent and creative. Each bomb had been a challenge and deserved respect, time and focus. He'd been a leader of men, then a teacher of US officers which had boosted his morale and his status. Now he found the prospect of the change a different kind of challenge and one where he had to wait to be told what to do and how to do it. It was hard to have to step away from the physical exertions and stop being a problem-solver with the resulting adrenaline rush you got after neutralising a deadly UXB. For two years he had lived it and breathed it. He missed the men's quick banter and the camaraderie of his section. He missed the important position he'd had which was recognised as a vital one. Now he was hidden away in an office.

But he had to face the fact he'd become less than enthusiastic about defuzing bombs and more aware of his fragility as time had passed. As each new day brought another dangerous job, which was then successfully completed, he knew his luck had been stretched like his nerves and he'd been one of the lucky ones. But it was still hard to accept the inevitability of the desk job.

He knew many would have given anything to be in that 'safe' job, the sort he had actually thought he might have had when he first signed up. Although he was fully recuperated he knew he had been more than fortunate to survive two years in bomb disposal and it had taken its toll, making him ill and draining him. You couldn't see the mental scars. They went deeper and lasted a lifetime.

John worked for Lieutenant General Sir J Robert Charles

KCB CMG DSO, a heroic soldier in WWI. General Charles had the honorary title of Chief Royal Engineer. He was the most senior serving officer and therefore he had advisory and ceremonial responsibilities. His job was to visit units and attend parades, and he was responsible for seeing the Corps policy maintained. It would have been his job also to keep the Colonel-in-Chief, the King, informed and maintain contact with engineer units throughout the Commonwealth. John would have helped plan and organise inspections, meetings and visits, checking and double-checking the transfer of that information and travel arrangements. He also attended the inspections of Royal Engineers Companies around the country, making sure everything ran smoothly – or else!

Captain Hannaford far left and General Charles inspecting troops preparing to go overseas

John eventually made the most of it. He had a positive outlook. He realised he was in a better place than most. The Blitz was over and the war had moved on. Everyone believed the war could be won now the US Army were putting their might behind the war effort in Europe and the Far East. He was privy to more information and news than he ever would have been if he'd returned to South Wales or even to the training of the US Bomb Disposaleers.

Gradually stories filtered through about the courageous and heroic acts of his colleagues in bomb disposal. It was both thrilling and chilling to hear what was going on because John understood fully the risks and the awful tension they underwent daily. Occasionally John was called upon to explain the intricacies of the bomb workings and the different methods of tackling each fuze. He explained clearly with the knowledge he'd built up. His clarity of memory of those precise steps remained with him to the end of his life.

When John got together with his BD colleagues they discussed many reports of bravery. One of the earliest that was always a topic of conversation was of courageous Captain Max Blaney and his team. He was an intelligent, debonair, careful and well-respected officer. He'd already disarmed and removed many UXBs when he was sent to oversee the extraction of an unexploded bomb from a vast crater in Romford Road, East London. He had taken every precaution before hoisting the 250kg weapon out of the ground.

Its two detonating fuzes had been identified. One was a clockwork time fuze with an 80-hour limit, the other a motion-sensitive fuze with a 60-hour shelf life. As several days had passed between the bomb landing and the team reaching the site, it seemed that both were now harmless.

Max Blaney used a clockstopper, a newly invented device that clamped around the bomb, and used a magnetic field to jam the time fuze's mechanism.

He had hoped to use another innovation, a steam steriliser that dissolved and pumped out the bomb's explosive, but the lorry bringing it had got stuck in traffic. It was Friday the 13th. Captain Blaney decided to proceed without it.

He had to remove the clockstopper briefly to get the hoist around the bomb, but as the fuzes had expired this did not appear risky.

When the bomb was hauled up from its tomb, Blaney stepped forward to steady it.

As he did so, there was a huge explosion. In a microsecond, the bomb was transformed into a searing blast of thunderous noise, white-hot heat and blinding light that tore outwards, destroying everything in its path.

Max Blaney, the eight men who had been pulling on the rope, and a watching policeman were all killed.

The day after the explosion, a button from the policeman's uniform was found embedded deep in a door frame further down the street. Very little else that was found was so easily recognisable.

It later transpired that the cold of the frozen earth had prolonged the battery life of the motion-sensitive fuze. The act of tugging the bomb out of its hole had caused it to detonate.

There was a clampdown on such stories. Their job was

classified as top secret, but even so stories like this had still found their way to South Wales. John remembered calming his men and himself in those early days when reports of whole teams being wiped out filtered through. They talked of luck and some of the men, being superstitious, had remarked on the unlucky date. Max Blaney was so experienced and particular it seemed really bad luck. It was a sobering tale.

John particularly liked to follow the exploits of Colonel Stuart Archer as a fellow BD officer in South Wales. As his BD unit was working just along the coast from John's, he'd heard a lot about him. His great courage was well known. He was awarded the George Cross for his sustained courage in bomb disposal work and for providing the War Office with different types of German weapon components at a time when very little was known about them. King George VI invested Col. Archer with the George Cross on October 21, 1941 at Buckingham Palace.

After one bomb blew up while a detail of soldiers, solely armed with picks and shovels, was on its way to excavate it, Archer telephoned his wife to say that he was going to get a place nearby for her to live because it did not look as if he was going to last very long.

John's favourite story was about the oil refineries in September 1940. After a heavy raid on the National Oil Refineries at Skewen, near Swansea, a huge fire started in six oil storage tanks. Archer and his section, guided by fires and smoke that could be seen 20 miles away, arrived at 10 am. Close to the large gasometer-like tanks containing fuel there were four unexploded 250 kg bombs in a straight line.

In Archer's own words, 'the one to tackle was right by the side of one of the oil tanks. It had broken through the concrete base of the tank itself. Only 50 or so yards away an oil tank was on fire so the heat was intense and the excitement terrific.'

The team began digging a shaft wide enough to enable Archer to get to the fuze. After an hour of digging, the nearest of the three remaining bombs exploded. Two hours later, another blew up. They continued digging and on uncovering the bomb, discovered that the fuze head had sheared off, making it impossible to tell what type of fuze they were dealing with.

Ordering his team to take cover, Archer unscrewed the base plate of the bomb, dug out the explosive powder with a trowel, and exposed the fuze pocket. "By getting my arm down inside the bomb, I was able to hold the fuze pocket and with brute force and bloody ignorance bang it back and forth until I got the whole thing free."

Archer exposed some wires sticking up out of the fuze pocket. Pulling on these with a pair of pliers, he found the clock for the type 17 fuze. It was still ticking. Peering down the tube, he could see another strange object. He tried to pull or shake it out, but with no success. Eventually, he managed to tap it out on a rail, but as he did so there came the sharp crack of a detonator. The sound he heard was the firing of a ZUS-40 anti-withdrawal device. It would seem that some water had found its way into the damaged fuze pocket and dampened the explosive charge in the device.

He commented: 'I had our lovely prize, a 17 fuze and the first ZUS-40 to come out in one piece. Lots of people had pulled them out before but they had been blown up, whereas I hadn't. This was luck, luck, luck.'

The fuze and the anti-handling device were sent to the War Office scientists and provided vital information for the bomb disposal teams.

John met Stuart Archer whilst attending meetings and training in London and again in the 1960s. John arranged for him to come to meet him at his daughter Jill's home in London when John was staying with her family. Both men were in their eighties and spent their time reminiscing about their years in WWII.

Colonel Stuart Archer survived the war, also enjoying a successful career as an architect, and lived until he was 100 years old, dying a few months before John thus sadly making John call himself the 'Last Man Standing'.

John's knowledge didn't help with his superior's questions when reports of Butterfly Bombs started to filter through. Luckily he hadn't come across those, though he'd heard of them in training, but nor had experienced Bomb Disposal officer Eric Wakeling when he was called upon to go to clear and defuze them. He'd spent 26 years of his life defuzing unexploded ordnance within the Royal Engineers. It was to be his greatest military contribution.

Butterfly Bombs were first used on Grimsby by the German Luftwaffe in June 1943. Lt. Eric Wakeling was among the first to risk his life defuzing the small but deadly bombs.

Entering Grimsby, he was met with a scene of death and destruction. The town had been virtually paralysed as more than 3,000 of the new bombs had been dropped. They were everywhere: cinema projection rooms, gutters, hedges, even sewers. If you could think of a place, there was a bomb there. They were the first type of anti-personnel cluster bomb to be developed and specifically intended to kill and maim ordinary people. Fourteen people died in the raid but 43 directly afterwards as people emerged from their homes or shelters. Bombs continued to be found for years after.

The farmers in Lincolnshire were reluctant to operate their harvesters, as their fields of cereal were still full of the little bombs so they had tanks to tow the reapers. There were many casualties, the saddest perhaps being the death of a young boy. His headstone bears the simple inscription:

Frank Childs,
Aged 9
Killed by Enemy Action.

Over seven days, work was carried out on an unprecedented scale. This not only included the disposal of Butterfly Bombs, but for Eric Wakeling, as an officer, it was also his job to dispose of conventional bombs.

According to the Royal Engineers' Bomb Disposal records, he was responsible for the clearance of more of these devices than anyone else. He was hailed a bomb disposal genius.

The speed at which the bombs were cleared, thanks to Wakeling and his men, plus the great secrecy which surrounded the clearing, meant that it was the last time the enemy used them on such a large scale. If they had known how disruptive and deadly they had been, they would certainly have used them again.

Lieutenant Colonel Eric Wakeling was hailed as a World War II hero. He was a much-admired colleague of John's and appeared with him in the Channel 4 documentaries, *Danger UXB*.

What had happened to Ken Revis, another hero officer and an experienced one, chilled John to the bone, when in September 1943 he heard of his awful accident. It reminded him immediately of his own men of 16 Company killed on a Pembrokeshire beach when he'd heard they'd been wiped out.

Ken Revis and his men had been sent to clear the mines off Brighton Pier. Whilst removing the booby traps they blew up in his face. The story goes that the nurse who found him badly injured had put a sheet over his face but he called out to remove it because 'I'm not dead yet,' he said.

He was taken to East Grinstead Hospital and required endless plastic surgery to remake his broken face and body. He became an inspiration to all, especially those with similar injuries from bomb blasts like himself. King George VI presented him with an MBE for his courage.

Many years later when attending a reunion, John met Ken, his wartime hero, who went on to have a full and varied career, helping others at St Dunstan's for the rehabilitation of soldiers blinded in the line of duty. He then was sent to India where he continued his inspirational support for soldiers who'd lost their sight there. After returning home, he trained as a solicitor. He was a remarkable man and also a well-known celebrity on radio and in the media.

Another inspiring story that was reported in the newspapers was about the siege of Malta. The spirit and determination of the islanders reminded John of how Londoners survived when they were besieged in the Blitz. Many years later, John and Joyce Hannaford visited Malta. He had his photo taken at the church at Mosta where the congregation were saved when an enemy bomb fell on the church, crashing through the roof and landing in the aisle without exploding. It is still celebrated to this day as a miracle UXB. Although the original bomb was removed and exploded offshore, another similar defuzed 250kg bomb replaced it and remains in the church for all to see.

All John's personal heroes remained in his thoughts, appearing in his notes regularly throughout his life, particularly Lieutenant Douglass, his mentor, teacher and father figure.

Lieutenant Walker who made the deadly error when training him and his men remained in his thoughts all his days because of a last request unfulfilled and a message of love undelivered.

But uppermost in his memories were his ordinary sappers. They were true heroes, he said. His team of men survived many dangerous jobs whilst John was their commanding officer before he left to go to London. They trained hard and worked hard. They had nerves of steel. They were wonderful, spirited lads and worked with great good humour. Their voices haunted him. Could he have saved them? It was a question he asked himself often.

Their luck ran out.

CHAPTER X
BUILDING FOR THE FUTURE

After being demobbed, John was given three months' leave. He spent those glorious days, after the war had been won, back in Devon, staying with his mother and father at the London Inn in Shaldon across from Teignmouth.

He spent his time on the beach or in the bay on-board a little boat with an outboard motor fishing in the clear waters of the estuary. Evenings were spent in the bar either playing the piano, smoking, drinking beer and singing their favourite songs, or telling and retelling the stories of their wartime exploits. Some now sounded too far-fetched to be real and he'd never have dared tell the stuff before; others he couldn't share yet. But it was the same for all the returning local soldiers, bruised and battle-worn. But at least they were back. So many had not returned and those who had were still recovering, and there were some who never would.

There was a lot to be thankful for and a rousing 'Welcome home' ceremony on the village green for all the returning soldiers where they were each presented with a commemorative wallet with a £5 note inside. There were flags up and bunting, and a band playing. The London Inn, his parents' pub, also on the green, did a roaring trade. It was a fine celebration. The villagers tried not to think of those lost or still missing. It was a jolly occasion.

Once his leave was over he returned to the Ministry of Works as Assistant Architect and continued his training to gain his qualifications. He had moved to digs in Chiswick, where he met Joyce. They were both keen dancers. Music was a great healer and everyone wanted to move on, though there were still restrictions, coupons for food and the sound of building and clearing of rubble. There was a positive and optimistic feeling in the air.

Joyce lived in her family home above her parents' shoe repairers, also in Chiswick. She was an attractive, petite young woman with beautiful hair and a lovely smile. They made a handsome couple and photos show them in the height of fashion, happy to pose for their photographs. Joyce made her clothes and was a fine dressmaker.

Joyce

Joyce had first been married in 1940 aged nineteen and had been widowed. She had been 24 and eight months pregnant when her first husband had died at Arnhem in Belgium in 1944. Jackie was born soon after. When John and Joyce married he adopted Jackie as his own daughter. Jill was born the year after.

When his work took him to Reading they had their first house built to John's plans and specifications, and they lived there until 1964.

He continued to be linked to bombs and worked at Aldermaston in Berkshire, designing the Atomic Weapons Establishment. He later said he really didn't like being there. And didn't like bombs at all.

Due to his promotion as a Senior Architect for the South of England he worked on military establishments from Chatham to Portsmouth, and as far west as North Devon. The family moved to a large house in Hastings. Jackie had grown up and remained in Reading for her work. Jill was still at school, so moved with her parents.

John's greatest and most satisfying job was his last as Senior Architect and was the winning design and planning of the Dover Coastguard building opened by Prince Charles.

In 1983 they retired to Bexhill and to the seafront flat they shared until the end of their lives. Joyce and John loved their flat with its views out to sea and across to Beachy Head and their walks along the seafront or just sitting on the promenade.

Friends and neighbours remember them sitting on their favourite seat and as they approached, John would always get up and take off his hat in welcome. 'He was a true gentleman,' they said. But if someone was parked in the wrong place outside their flat, he soon let them know.

Joyce gave up work to become homemaker, designing and making the girls' clothes as they grew up. She studied flower arranging and learnt to drive at 50. She also learnt to play golf and won many local club tournaments at the Highwoods Golf Club in Bexhill. She was better than John. His daughters laughed, telling me, 'That's why he gave it up.'

They both loved music and shared a love of opera and ballet. Joyce and John's friends described them as both strong characters with a traditional marriage, which lasted over 60 years. Joyce told her friend she was pleased she hadn't known John when he was in bomb disposal. She said she'd have been too worried as it was such a dangerous job.

He never discussed anything to do with bomb disposal until nearly 40 years later when he became a member of his much-loved Royal Engineers Bomb Disposal Officers Club and started to share memories with those who'd been through the same experiences.

Retired John with bomb

In his nineties he was able to retell his often-painful stories when interviewed by the Imperial War Museum for their records. Maybe at last there was an opportunity to revisit those memories buried for so long. John needed to talk and wanted to continue the interviews for longer. He needed that therapy much sooner, but dismissed Post-Traumatic Stress Disorder (PTSD) when Jackie mentioned it to him.

Jill described how her mother Joyce complained that she was all 'bomb disposalled out'. A neighbour, trying to explain about John, said, 'It was all he talked about whenever they spoke. It was always uppermost in his thoughts and the first subject of any conversation.'

John lived a full and interesting life and had a successful career as an architect. He had the most peaceful of pastimes and spent hours producing many beautiful watercolours. He was a happy family man, a husband to a 'wonderful wife', a proud father and father-in-law, extremely proud grandfather and great-grandfather.

He gained riches beyond compare and had fulfilled the family motto his father quoted so often as he grew up: 'Riches to rags, rags to riches'.

He was still not satisfied. His men remained in his thoughts. Their forgotten acts of bravery gnawed away at him until the day he died. He left them to that dangerous job of dismantling mines. Did he feel he'd abandoned his men? He remarked that maybe he could have taken a different course.

In *Danger UXB* John Hannaford told the author M.J. Jappy that his time as a Bomb Disposal officer was 'an unforgettable, seminal period of his life. Looking back over my long lifetime, there has been nothing else like it. It's so vivid in my mind now. The strange thing is the ability of the mind to remember voices. The sergeant who called to me at the Usk bomb – I can hear his voice now. And my wonderful men, the sappers who were killed – I can hear their voices now. It's very emotive and it is something very, very powerful in my life.'

In John's notes dated 25th January 2014, a year before he died, he wrote,

'Although many years have passed since my service in REBD the memories remain vivid, particularly of wartime colleagues and so many incidents that remain etched in my mind. Service colleagues of all ranks that just got on with the job in hand seemingly oblivious to the all too real danger and particularly of those who didn't make it. I think of their families, bereaved and still left to this day wondering just exactly what happened and what were the circumstances.'

Whilst being interviewed John sadly looked at the fading photographs of his team saying, 'It gets to you more as the years go by. Most of the team perished, the majority not in defuzing enemy bombs but clearing British mines from beaches. There was some kind of fairness about being killed by an enemy bomb. You expected it. But we lost so many good men to our own mines. To lose your life on a peaceful beach to a British-laid mine seemed the ultimate obscenity of war.'

A description of the immense and often deadly job of clearing the mines is given in Major Arthur Hogben's book, *Designed to Kill*.

Searching was the key word in perhaps the most dangerous and trying single task to be given to the Royal Engineer bomb disposal units in 1943. It was the clearance of some 2,000 separate minefields laid on the beaches and clifftops around the coast of Great Britain as a defence against threatened invasion. Initially the task was to clear selected beaches so that Allied troops could practise their own invasion techniques, but the task quickly grew to include all the 350,000 anti-tank mines laid on British beaches and the exits from them. Technically this was not a bomb disposal task, although it was given to bomb disposal units. The story of the work of all the officers, non-commissioned officers, sappers, prisoners of war and eventually ex-prisoners of war deserves a full-length book of its own. 151 men were killed on this task between 1943 and 1947.

Major Hogben states, 'and to the many hundreds of unnamed and frequently unremembered men who worked in constant threat of death even when for others the war was over their work should be remembered.' Now and in the future, just as long as weapons designed to kill are left in the ground posing a threat to life and limb, bomb disposal men or women will continue to do the dangerous job of searching, finding and disposing of mines.

The difficulties of the WWII mine clearance task were enormous. The mines had been laid in great haste in 1940, with the result that the minefield records, although showing the general areas in which the mines were laid, contained very little reliable information as to the exact position of the mines and in some cases even the total numbers laid. In one classic case the map used was an unamended 1906 edition. Even if the exact position of all the mines had been shown, there were many instances where the action of wind and tide over the years had altered the whole topography of the area. Mines laid a few inches below the surface of the sand or shingle often became buried deep beneath dunes of sand or banks of shingle. It was not unusual to find that mines had been carried by storms to points far along the coast from where they were originally laid. Similarly, mines laid on clifftops had, as the cliff was eroded, slid to the bottom of the cliff and either been buried under tons of material or washed out to sea, only to be returned to another beach which may already have been cleared.

The most modern instruments then available were used to locate the whereabouts of these mines, but many were buried beyond their effective range. Furthermore, the instruments were liable to indicate the presence of a mine which, when uncovered, turned out to be nothing more dangerous than a large tin or other metallic object with which the beaches had become strewn following the war.

Finally, the mines themselves had suffered from long years of corrosion. One of the most numerous mines to be laid was the anti-tank mine known as the B Type C. This depended for its action upon a pressure of 50 lb (22.7kg) on the edge, or 100 lb (45.4kg) on the centre of its domed top, which reversed a simple, bow-shaped spring. This spring drove a striker onto a cartridge cap and so fired the mine. After years of corrosion the bow spring became weaker and its supports less strong. This left the mine in a highly sensitive condition and instead of the intended activation pressure the weight of a man's foot or even a handful of sand could be sufficient to set off the 251 lb (11.4kg) of explosive contained in the mine.

Various forms of mechanical equipment were used to clear the beaches and cliff edges. One method was to carry out a surface sweep with mine-detectors, then to use armoured bulldozers to scrape off a layer of sand or shingle equal to the effective depth of the search instrument and then resweep and continue this until the required depth had been cleared. Another method was to use powerful water jets to clear away the accumulation of sand and shingle until the mines were exposed. Whatever method was used in the way of mechanical devices, the final search had always to be carried out by men armed only with mine-detectors and complete faith in the other members of their team.

The work of sweeping for and clearing beach mines must inevitably be a very slow and deliberate operation. Any attempt to hurry was all too likely to be attended by fatal results. This work tested a unit's morale to its limit. It was tedious, dangerous and, except when a mine was recovered or someone was killed, boring in the extreme. Between 1943 and 1948 a total of 1,986 minefields consisting of 338,500 mines were cleared. This left eleven small areas, the last of which was cleared in 1972.

Training areas are still being cleared to this day. Mines still turn up on beaches. Today's soldiers may have improved detection, but they still have great risk to overcome. Their job is still a dangerous one.

The 151 who were killed between 1943 and 1948 should be thanked in military terms for making the ultimate sacrifice. They also deserve public recognition. It needs to happen now. John wanted families to know and to celebrate their heroic bomb disposal ancestor's courageous wartime work.

CHAPTER XI
CATSFIELD: A LOCAL SUSSEX MYSTERY

The mystery began to unfold when John and his wife Joyce visited St. Laurence Church, in Catsfield, East Sussex, in September 2003. In their eighties they still enjoyed exploring the Sussex countryside. They bought the church history booklet and browsed through the ancient building and churchyard. As they read the history, they were surprised to learn that in the churchyard were buried two Royal Engineer Bomb Disposal personnel. Of course they were keen to see the grave with the memorial stone. Apparently, the men had been well known in the village and had both lost their lives whilst defuzing a bomb.

Sadly the stone was hidden under bushes and in a sad state. John was upset and angry and was determined to get it cleaned up. He also wanted to find out how they had died.

He was well aware of the dangers of defuzing unexploded bombs or UXB. He had lost many good comrades in just that way. This is the account of the local mystery.

The date on the headstone puzzled him: it was 1944. He thought that any bombs that had dropped would have been earlier in the war.

John returned the next day to Catsfield to see if he could find anyone who remembered either the air battle or the location of the bomb incident, and he came away disappointed, as everyone who might have remembered had either died or moved away.

Finding out more became a real challenge and John wrote that he was not deterred. He visited libraries and museums, rummaged through old newspapers looking for any mention of the matter, and talked to as many people as he could. At first, he met a series of dead ends. Then a local librarian told him that Second World War records were kept at the County Library in Lewes. It was there that he began to unravel the story.

He found that an RAF report dated 11.9.40 states:

'6/KG1 Heinkel He 111H-2 (5364) both engines disabled by fighter attacks during sortie to bomb London Docks. Dumped bombs and force-landed at Broomhill Farm, Camber 4.40 p.m. where crew set fire to the aircraft. Uffz. B. Hansen, Uffz. K. Markert, Uffz. J. Krall and Gefr. G Wilhelm captured unhurt. Uffz. H. Widhopf captured wounded. Aircraft B4+RW were a write-off.'

He knew the date the bombs dropped and it was also confirmed that the bombs had been dumped on a farm in Udimore.

John continued to research the story and asked a local farmer friend about the bomb incident, and asked him if he knew of any farmers in the Udimore area. Luckily he did and even knew the family who in 1944 were operating Billingham Farm.

With this information, John made contact with surviving family members who showed an immediate interest in an event, which 60 years on still held vivid memories but had left them with many unanswered questions.

With the help of the family, at last the long-lost story began to emerge. It was a poignant tale.

As recorded in the Royal Air Force report in September 1940, three Heinkel bombers had been turned back from their intended raid to London. They ditched their bombs over East Sussex, on the edge of Romney Marsh. This area would have been identified in advance as a potential site for an emergency landing, or at least for dumping bombs so that the reduced load would make it possible for the planes to make it to home territory. And so it happened on that late summer's day that two of the planes crash-landed within sight of each other on Broomhill Farm at Camber near Rye. The crews left their planes and set fire to them. Eight Germans were quickly captured; one was wounded, and two others had been killed. John found out that they became prisoners of war in Canada. How could they possibly have known that, three and a half years later, one of their bombs would do what it was designed to do, to kill the Bomb Disposal men who tried to defuze it?

Three of the bombs which had been dropped on Backdoor Field were made safe and removed at the time in 1940. Three other bombs fell on muddy ground. The Bomb Disposal personnel found that digging for these bombs only made them sink further into the mud. Since the Bomb Disposal units were busy elsewhere at the time, and it was considered that the bombs were no immediate threat and they were abandoned.

By 1944, however, the Ministry of Agriculture wanted to see the field returned to its agricultural use to help with the war effort.

Two of the bombs were successfully defuzed, but the farm owner was naturally reluctant to begin cultivating until the only remaining bomb was neutralised and removed. Royal Engineers Lieutenant George Cunningham and Sergeant George Mack were instructed to remove the remaining UXB.

They were stationed about twelve miles away at a large house called Burntwood near Catsfield where No 20 Bomb Disposal Company, Royal Engineers, had its base. Visits to the village pub were no doubt the reason for the two men as being 'well known in the village'. Lt. Cunningham of Irish extraction and aged 33 was born in Ohio, USA, and Sgt. Mack aged 26 was born in Ayr, Scotland. Both were unmarried.

John could imagine that the two young men would not have felt defuzing the third bomb to be a difficult job. The bomb lay in a peaceful rural setting. They were not in a hurry, nor were they in the midst of a bombing raid, as so often happened with bomb disposal operations. Besides, by that time, bomb disposal teams knew a great deal about German fuzes, and were trained and equipped to deal with them.

Sgt. Mack and his squad of sappers arrived onsite, dug the shaft and eventually exposed the bomb. Then Lt. Cunningham was seen to arrive by car from No. 20 Bomb Disposal Company. It would have been his job to actually defuze the bomb.

John's own wartime experiences told him that Lt. Cunningham would have probably approached the bomb assuming that after lying for three and half years under eighteen feet of waterlogged soil, time would have done its work on the 250kg bomb. He must have been reasonably sure that the bomb would be safe. It wasn't.

According to Dennis Crouch, who was a young farm worker at the time, Sgt. Mack stood at the top, looking down, while Lt. Cunningham climbed into the hole. He quickly found that the bomb had a No. 17 clockwork fuze, for the number would have been clearly visible on the face of the fuze. But unfortunately under it was the 'ZUS-40' booby trap (short for 'Zusatz' in German, meaning additional device).

John thought this should have been anticipated for five of the six bombs dumped on the farm had already been defuzed successfully, and it was well known by Bomb Disposal personnel that out of a typical load of six 250kg bombs, one would probably have an anti-handling fuze, which would operate whether the bomb was armed or not. There were special techniques for the safe disposal of such potentially dangerous fuzes.

John never knew why they weren't used.

When Lt. Cunningham withdrew the fuze, a powerful spring trigger shot into a percussion cap and set off the main bomb charge, and as Dennis Crouch recalls, there was a huge explosion followed by a towering column of black smoke.

The horrified sappers were seen to quickly load their equipment and speed away to their base.

Searchers found nothing more of the two than a shredded pound note in the woods.

Sadly, as D-Day was imminent, the customary funeral services were apparently never held for the two men.

Being familiar with Second World War bomb disposal techniques, John was able to tell the family what had almost certainly happened on that May day in 1944.

After so many years, at last they could understand the bravery of the young men who died in an effort to make their farm safe.

As the result of John's research and many enquiries, it was decided to arrange a memorial service for Lt. Cunningham and Sgt. Mack, fittingly and precisely on the 60th anniversary of their deaths. It was also possible to name and to remember the bravery of the RAF pilots who prevented the Heinkels from reaching their targets in London. Records had made it possible to identify them as Squadron Leader R.H.A. Leigh, Flying Officer R.W. Oxspring and Sgt. D.A.C. Hunt of 66 Squadron, Flight Lieutenant A.E. Wright of 92 Squadron, and Pilot Officer E.S. Lock of 41 Squadron.

The tribute to the two BD officers killed at Catsfield

It was at 2.35 p.m. on May 6th, 2004, 60 years to the day, the hour and the minute from the time when the bomb exploded, that Captain John Hannaford and 40 people and press gathered at St. Laurence Church, Catsfield. Led by standard-bearers from the Army and the RAF, they proceeded to the dual headstone of Lt. Cunningham and Sgt. Mack, now pristine white and cleared of the shrubs that had enveloped it. There were no bodies there, of course. An exploding bomb seldom left any remains. However, it was usual to take sandbags of earth from the crater, approximately the weight of the deceased, place in a coffin, and send to the bereaved family for burial. The families of Lt. Cunningham and Sgt. Mack were denied even this focal point for their grief.

The Rector of St. Laurence Church conducted a moving ceremony during which poppy wreaths were laid. When the bugler sounded the Last Post, it rang out across the quiet countryside accompanied by the musical song of a blackbird. John wondered that it was perhaps the last sound heard by the two soldiers going about their dangerous work.

John felt a strong bond with the two men. After being forgotten for so many years he felt they were finally remembered and honoured by the villagers of Catsfield who knew them so well. Their names have been added to the year's mind list in the church so that on the closest Sunday to May 6th each year, their names are mentioned in the prayers at Parish Communion.

I visited the cemetery at 2.35 on May 6th, 2016, six months after John died and 72 years later. The day was bright with spring sunshine and thundery showers. A carpet of primroses, violets and bluebells and lush green moss led up to the pure white memorial headstone. A golden Christmas decoration lay tucked in the grass at the base of the stone. I hoped that Lt. Cunningham and Sgt. Mack's familes would visit one day in that special place to remember their brave young men.

The Royal Engineers insignia is carved into the white stone with the names of the two men.

Lieutenant G.K.O'B Cunningham
Royal Engineers
6th May 1944 Age 32

Greater love
Hath no man than this
That a man lay down his
Life for his friends

Sergeant G.L. Mack
Royal Engineers
6th May 1944 Age 25

It was a peaceful Sussex scene. The fields surrounding the small country cemetery were beautiful under the budding trees. A woodpecker flew, swooping a wavy flight path across the grassy banks, calling out its tribute. Like a salute!

We will remember them.

CHAPTER XII
FAMILY HEROES

Uncle Alex's collection

Thanks to researching Captain John Hannaford I also discovered my family had unexpected links with bomb disposal and mine clearance. When I started to share his unfolding story about his dangerous wartime job, it opened up a whole new conversation with my mum and dad and revealed a forgotten chapter in our family. My mum hadn't forgotten! She has a great memory and vast knowledge of our family history and immediately said, 'Don't you remember Uncle Alex was in bomb disposal and lasted the whole war?' He was actually my grandfather's brother, my great-uncle, but I had to confess I had forgotten. I was in my teens when he died and don't remember hearing about his war service. My mum also said he didn't talk about it either, just as John hadn't shared his stories for most of his life.

The following week when I visited she'd found his photos. There was also a wallet with money still in it and a few pieces of German wartime memorabilia, and the two incendiary bombs he'd brought back for his mother, my great-grandmother. Wartime souvenirs now safely defuzed of course. Lots of soldiers returned with them.

Maybe John Hannaford and my Great-Uncle Alex's paths crossed and they met somewhere in training. I certainly hope so. The coincidence in those early months was another surprise and good piece of news. The family connection enthused me even more. The momentum continued.

My dad sadly passed away whilst I have been writing John's story, but we had some very special moments discussing it and it jogged his memories of growing up in Glasgow and cycling to the docks the day after bombing raids with his friends hunting bomb-sites for shrapnel. A mother's nightmare, we agreed! He had quite a collection, he said. He still sounded peeved that his mother had got rid of it when they moved to Stranraer, back to where she grew up, to the coast, to get away from the fumes of the city.

Sapper Alexander Murray grew up in the Rhins of Galloway in South West Scotland. He served his time in Belgium and France and also here in England defuzing bombs in and around Luton in Bedfordshire very near where my parents moved to, relocating from Scotland. I found out from Steve Venus that 184 Company had trained not far from where he lived in Pinner, London, and my mum recalls hearing about him training on Hampstead Heath. Steve was fascinated to read his training exercise book, carefully written with instructions and diagrams.

Once I received John's Records I was able to find another link. John's Company were sent to the South Coast to prepare for D-Day, as were 184 Company.

Great Uncle Alex, bottom right

Great-Uncle Alex is on the front row on the right of this group photo. It's unusual as it's taken in work clothes, not dress uniform. It's quite informal. His team have just been digging. It seems more relaxed and is exactly how John described looking after they'd completed a job all covered in mud and often wet through, but happy they'd survived another dangerous job defuzing an enemy bomb. You can just make out the bomb disposal badge on the corporal's arm.

I am now the proud owner of two of these arm badges given to me by Steve Venus and Lieutenant Colonel Rod MacArthur. I also purchased the medals John would have received, but he told his family he had thrown them in the bin as his secretary received the same medals. His daughter Jill said he felt so badly let down. Bomb Disposal were not recognised with a separate medal for their dangerous war effort and still haven't been. That is what John, his colleagues and many others felt should have happened. He felt it was a great unfairness.

Sadly Great-Uncle Alex died of a heart attack in his fifties, a relatively young man. He never married, though my mum heard he'd courted a girl in the war, but she had eventually married his captain. In his wallet with two Belgian banknotes and a 1000 German Reichsbanknote are cards, which hopefully helped him recover. One is for the Esperia Bar in Brussels, welcoming Allied troops with music and girls to come and be their guests, and the other a family to contact. I hoped he'd had a really good time.

As a young girl my mum remembered writing a weekly letter to her Uncle Alex when she visited her grandmother each Sunday. Sadly, none of those letters remain.

1939 1945

Welcome Home from the People of the Parish of Kirkmaiden to

Alexander Murray

for your service during the Wor
War 1939~1945.

We record with all sincerity our gratitude for your devoted service to the nation.

We are proud that our sons and daughters were ready to make sacrifices when called upon to uphold the cause of Freedom Justice and Truth.

We thank God for your safe return.

Welcome home

When Mum produced the Uncle Alex 'Welcome home' certificate I could remember seeing it on the wall in my great-grandmother's sitting room when we visited her. She was obviously very proud of him and no doubt glad he got back home safely. Not surprisingly, I wasn't allowed to touch the incendiary bombs on the floor next to the fireplace, but I have now inherited them and Steve Venus has assured me they are safe and he has a fine collection of them himself. They were produced in 1936. 'A good year,' Steve remarked. Like a fine wine, I thought.

The most amazing piece of memorabilia is Uncle Alex's damaged hat badge. It has a hole and nick out of it where a tiny piece of shrapnel had sliced through it just millimetres or so from his head. It would have whistled by and probably made him duck for cover. He was a lucky man, too. I suppose everyone who lasted the war was. I remember my grandfather and Mum discussing his luck but I think they were talking about him winning at bingo, not his wartime exploits. After we moved south to Hertfordshire from South West Scotland, Alex would visit his brother, my grandfather, who'd moved with us. I can remember his softly spoken Scottish accent and his gentle humour.

Badge with hole

Our talk of wartime bombs and narrow escapes prompted my dad, whose memory was failing him and who was so weak he rarely walked unaided, to get up from his chair and disappear out of the room. Mum and I just stopped, frozen to the spot, surprised beyond words. Then we heard the outside door open and close. That was even more of a surprise. He hadn't willingly been outside for weeks. He felt the cold so much. What was going on? When he returned, a few moments later, he came straight to me and handed over a heavy, irregular and jagged chunk of metal, which filled my palm, and he said to me, 'It's shrapnel from a bomb. I found it in the garden.'

Dad's present

I was both amazed and touched. Mum and I listened as he tried to explain how bombs had been dropped on the nearby railway line between London and Cambridge. I checked out his story with his great friend Albert, also a Royal Engineer, who remembered bombs dropping near Ashwell and Morden station. One must have exploded, sending its shards of splintered shrapnel over a wide area and landing in our garden a couple of hundred metres away. After all his foraging for the pieces of shrapnel as a boy in Glasgow, he'd recognised it right away when he'd been digging. They'd lived there over 50 years. Goodness knows when he uncovered it, but it was many years before and he'd remembered exactly where he'd put it in his shed and treasured it.

The more I learn about bombs and their construction and the resulting mutilation and deaths, the ingenious science behind their development and the vast and ever-increasing expense, the more I can't understand the brutality and stupidity of their use.

John with all his added knowledge agreed and said, 'It was stupid.'

I can appreciate the luck that he and his colleagues would say again and again played a key part in their safe passage through the war and in avoiding injury from their blasts. It was a miracle there were so many who survived.

That potentially destructive and deadly fragment was Dad's last gift to me and it is here on the table in front of me. Its weight still shocks me as do its cruel, sharp edges made by the force of explosion. It could have ripped someone apart, and when I handle its rusty mass it reminds me of the horrific damage it could have done. But this fragment is truly special, a relic of war from my dad who was a gentle, kind and peace-loving man. It connects me to him through shared memories from the past. I know I will keep it forever.

Great-Uncle Alex is our family hero. It is wonderful to remember him in John's book about other ordinary men who joined up, not expecting that job.

My dad spent most of his last days dozing in his chair. On another occasion, as my mum and I chatted about my writing and unearthing more wartime events and following John's story, he suddenly spoke, telling me, 'Your great-grandfather served on a minesweeper in the Mediterranean in WWI.' It was unbelievable as his words were now few and far between and he said this clearly enough for us both to understand.

Again John's story had transported him back to his youth, to when he proudly listened to his own grandfather's heroic tales.

He was a fisherman and he remembered him bringing in his catch of the day. He remembered he loved the mackerel best. Dad then went back to sleep, leaving Mum to tell me more.

Great-Grandfather James Murdoch had been a merchant seaman. His ship had done the difficult and dangerous job of minesweeping to clear the seas off the coast of southern Italy, near Brindisi, in preparation for invasion by the Allies.

In WWII he was a fisherman out of Stranraer, but he would also meet and row in the pilots from their seaplanes who landed in the bay of Loch Ryan and were returning to their airbase at RAF Wig Bay nearby. The planes had the important job of detecting and bombing the German submarines attacking Allied shipping in the Atlantic.

I have a hazy, black and white photograph of my great-grandfather rowing out to a seaplane floating on the loch. That is quite a sight to see and another family story to remember – a fascinating tale for future generations of our family to know.

My wonderful family are like so many others disappearing into the mists of time, unless something happens to bring their stories and history alive, and then we discover heroes and write it down for posterity.

I will forever be in Captain John Hannaford's debt.

AN UNEXPECTED BOOK

Thank you for reading Captain Hannaford's remarkable story. He was one of many who performed that perilous job of bomb disposal. Unlike many of them, he survived to eventually share his tale. But when he should have been enjoying his final days, he was angry and annoyed, irritated and still desperately wanting to be heard. He used his final interview with a local journalist to get his message out there. He still believed he could get the recognition the WWII R.E. Bomb Disposal men deserved for their dangerous, life-threatening work 75 years before.

I never expected to write a book but when I told a local author about finding a painting and being so fascinated by the artist I wanted to write about him, she said, 'There are stories out there waiting to be written and you have just found yours.'

I am grateful to local author Andrea Samuelson for that first conversation which supported me and spurred me on. I was naïve, of course, thinking I could write it quickly. I believed I should get it written in John Hannaford's centenary year. I almost managed. It was much harder than I ever imagined, but it has been worth every effort involved. It has been an amazing journey into the past, a quest, a challenge and an adventure all rolled into one.

I connected with John's painting immediately and was consumed with interest in the artist. Coincidences continued throughout the writing process. These kept me focused, as so much happened along the way. Writing stopped at times and it's like walking through treacle starting up again. I was able to look up at John's painting above my writing table to feel that first connection. The fire in his words continued to inspire me and was worth passing on. I was determined to help get what he wanted for others.

Andrea told me, 'Just write every day. You can edit after.'

My wonderful support network strengthened my resolve. Sharing was not easy. I was hesitant and scared of negative comments. But I was also driven in the end to tell John's important story, which will rise above any inefficiency in the technicalities of my writing and impress you, as it has me.

I plotted out a mind map then added to it as I learnt more. Visuals helped me. I pasted a large board with photos and another one for the USP, the unique selling point. Who might want to read the story? It will perhaps be those it reaches who might not want to read it at first that matter.

I certainly did not expect to write about bomb disposal. But its horror gripped me as recent terrorist bombs do when they hit the headlines. Bomb disposal officers and their teams are still at risk. It still happens and WWII bombs are still discovered and need defuzing.

By telling this story of heroism in WWII I hope that it can be recognised and remembered. The RE Bomb Disposal soldiers had little choice. John didn't like bombs at all, but he thought he was doing something worthwhile.

The research into his story was an unexpected treat. I didn't know it would be a puzzle to unravel and then piece together. It was exciting but often frustrating as well. It was even challenging deciphering John's notes or understanding the terminology of bomb disposal. But when a connection happened or a piece of story fell into place, it was truly thrilling.

One night whilst working late on the computer I again questioned: should I do this? Then it seemed the strangest thing happened. I appeared to get an answer.

It read, 'Make all the trumpet sounds or drum rolls, if you prefer.'

I stopped, incredulous. It was a positive message however it appeared. Described to me later as a 'happenstance'. After all that had occurred in such a short space of time, it didn't seem that improbable to me.

I could almost hear the fanfare. It was for John and his heroes.

His family's support was vital. They shared so much information. I had the visual evidence of his skills as a watercolourist. I was able to read what he'd experienced, even if they were on little scraps of paper sometimes written vertically up the margin to use every last bit of the surface. I saw him being interviewed and his enjoyment at having an audience was evident, his memory of those frightening experiences in WWII was fresh, even raw. I had been concerned that I might not like him when I saw him. But it was as if he were there in the room telling me his stories personally, his sense of humour shining through and his doggedness and passion about his past resolute. To hear his voice and see his mannerisms both in his seventies for the Danger UXB interviews then hear him as an elderly man in his nineties for the Imperial War Museum, his breathing more laboured, his speaking more measured and stilted, was a privilege. I began to feel I knew him really well. I was able to call him John, not Captain Hannaford. I wasn't being disrespectful.

The technical stuff was hard to get a grip of. I read the books suggested by Lt. Col. Rod MacArthur and Steve Venus, who has all the books that the Imperial War Museum stores. I found that out afterwards. I should have gone to Steve first, as he knew the Bomb Disposal authors personally and was a good friend to John. I pored over their words and their writing helped immensely, but I kept returning to reread John's notes. I missed things even after reading his notes several times. Sometimes I discovered he seemed to get things wrong, but communication was very different then. No television, no Internet and few telephones. I wanted to believe everything he said as he was there in the thick of it. My great-uncle's training notebook was invaluable. John would have used the same with the US Disposaleers. I wonder again if their paths crossed.

I was nervous about contacting the Royal Engineers. The very formality of the names and titles of people to contact was confusing and daunting. I pronounced Lieutenant wrong, the American way, so many times to my husband, he would shout, "Left!"

And I'd correct myself.

When I made visits to museums to research and asked questions about bombs or fuzes accompanied by my husband, men answered him, not me, until he said, 'It's my wife who is writing this story.' I suppose it's not normally an interest women might follow. Although it's mostly women I've told his story to so far and they appreciate the complexities and difficulties those early teams of bomb disposal men would have encountered as much as any man. There are now many women doing the job and they are as professional as their male colleagues and just as courageous in dealing with the challenging and dangerous aspects of bomb disposal.

I was reassured when I did make contact with the Royal Engineers that bomb disposal personnel are highly regarded in the modern British Army and there is a growing need for the services of the well-trained British Bomb Disposal units and their instructors. I was told that a new regiment is being formed in 2018, which will lead to two new Bomb Disposal Squadrons being formed. We are all aware that their presence is welcomed by the public and there is an expectation that if there is an explosive found, there is a team of experts nearby at all times to help deal with the situation. Recent troubles have highlighted their presence and there is always a need for trained soldiers willing to do that most dangerous job in our world today. Press photos of the searcher at the front of a BD unit with a detector, eyes peeled, 'eyes wide open', as John said, on the ground in front, makes you catch your breath at their bravery. It is surely the most intense and nerve-racking responsibility any young soldier is asked to do. I recently listened to a young RE officer say he had wanted to do it, but was too old when he joined the Army. How could you want to do that job? But thank goodness there are young people like him willing to take on that huge responsibility to protect us. I have great respect for that officer who shared his thoughts with me. Thank you, Ben.

WWII units were unprepared and therefore at greater risk. Their teams were overwhelmed by the job of clearing UXBs, but they did it and at a high cost. Everyone I've spoken to is incredulous of their courage carrying out those early assignments. Everyone also is shocked when you tell them they never were recognised for their considerable and sustained bravery dealing daily with their job for the six years of the war.

John wanted honour for his colleagues, dignity for all ranks and the recognition they deserved. He was one of the last. He still speaks out through these pages. He and they are no longer alive, but can still be honoured posthumously. Other deserving groups have recently been remembered in this way. Surely there is a sound case for these heroic WWII soldiers' families to receive a special medal for their immeasurable commitment to saving lives, homes, factories, hospitals and morale here at home in war-torn Britain.

I would have wanted him to be proud of this final plea and case for them. His story has opened my eyes wide to the bravery of those early teams. They never left these shores. They faced fear here and overcame it to do their job. Many died. Their job was vital. Winston Churchill recognised its importance. Some extremely brave individuals were awarded the George Cross or George Medal by King George VI, but what about every one of the officers and ordinary sappers digging down to find a ticking time bomb, then disarm it?

John's story made me cry. It shocked me and, unbelievably, it made me laugh as well. He introduced me to a completely different way of living, where every second counted and time stood still in a muddy hole. He was a charismatic gentleman and a good storyteller. His painting was his relaxation time, his therapy, yet it only started in his retirement. The painting of the De La Warr Pavilion was a wonderful treasure to find and an amazing link to an amazing man.

The Royal Engineers' Roll of Honour on their Bomb Disposal Branch of the Royal Engineers Association website is a fitting tribute. Officers like Lieutenant Walker and Lieutenant Douglass will not be forgotten. To the many others like them and those working today we must send our considerable appreciation and heartfelt thanks.

I respectfully request that Captain John Hannaford be remembered there, too.

John was saddened when visiting the Imperial War Museum in London. He said, 'After an extensive tour of all things WWII I asked an attendant – where could I find the bomb disposal display? He looked a bit confused, scratched his head and eventually said, "Oh! I think there is a German bomb on floor so-and-so." 'I was shocked and somewhat angry when I found the sole 250kg bomb almost hidden in a dark corner. Unbelievable but true.'

Visiting twice in the past year to carry out research, I admired the museum's excellent exhibits and expected to find more than John, but also had to search for evidence of their work. I also asked for help and the attendant couldn't give me any more information. I said I was writing a book about one of the last bomb disposal officers. He said that was a good thing and they should be remembered. It would have a significant impact if there were more references in displays and their importance in WWII history was highlighted. Young visitors, as well as those who still remember and appreciate their heroic and necessary work, should be able to witness this at our most prestigious wartime museum in the heart of London where so many lost their lives in the Blitz but so many more were saved by the bomb disposal teams.

John's passionate plea came through in his notes, conversations and his last interview. As he sat at his desk with his annotated family photograph album open before him, he reflected on his long and interesting life. He told the reporter, 'I'm just a lucky man.'

The pages were open at the photo of him as a young, inexperienced soldier.

He would have so many near misses, even believing he'd died and gone to Heaven on one occasion. He would witness some horrifying events, make split-second decisions to avoid being killed and suffer resulting stress, anxiety and physical injury, but to the very end he thought of the others.

'I can hear their voices as clear as if it were yesterday.'

He and his fellow Bomb Disposal officers and their teams deserve their place in history.

My greatest discovery and most powerful evidence that these brave men deserve creditation is from our greatest statesman, Winston Churchill, who asked that WWII Bomb Disposal teams be given the recognition they deserved for their highly dangerous work.

ARMISTICE DAY

The author and curator of Bexhill Museum

John lived close to Bexhill Museum. I visited there to see their WWII displays. I wondered if they knew about Captain John Hannaford. They didn't. After a conversation with the curator it was agreed that I could add my initial research and findings to their collection. I wanted his courageous effort and that of Bomb Disposal squads to be remembered in his home town.

Bexhill was bombed like other coastal towns. Maps showing where bombs fell can be examined at the museum. It's part of the story of the town during WWII.

The presentation was my first deadline and to take Captain John Hannaford's file on Armistice Day was particularly poignant, as he had died the previous year on that special day for our Armed Forces. Some of his friends laughed wryly and said it was just like him to do that. I'd like to think he tried especially hard to do just that, too.

I gave the research to Julian Porter, the Curator of Bexhill Museum, on the anniversary of his death in the Royal Engineer colours of gold and red.

John Dowling, who interviewed John Hannaford in October 2015, attended and he reported the event to the local *Bexhill Observer*. It was also reaching out online. John and his men were being remembered. That was satisfying. It was a start.

BIBLIOGRAPHY

Instructions for American Servicemen in Britain 1942 War Dept. Washington, DC

Danger UXB – James Owen

Danger UXB – M.J. Jappy

Designed to Kill – Major Arthur Hogben

Malta UXB – S.A.M. Hudson

Newton Abbot – John Bainbridge

The Lonely War – Lt. Col. Eric Wakeling

The Life and Times of Peter Mews – Dorothy Turcotte

Teignmouth at War Book 1 – Viv Wilson

Teignmouth at War Book 2 – Viv Wilson

The Book of Shaldon – Alec Collyer

True Stories of the Blitz – Henry Brook

World War II DK Eyewitness

You Only Blow Yourself Up Once – J. Frank Durham

OTHER SOURCES

Chapel Bay Fort and Museum, Angle, South Pembrokeshire

Danger UXB Channel 4 documentary

Danger UXB radio interview

IWM interview

Malta Story World War II film

History Society of Saundersfoot

Operation Jantzen maps and photographs, National Archives

Royal Engineers Bomb Disposal Officers Club
www.bombdisposalclub.org.uk

Steve Venus www.bombfuzecollectorsnet.com

The complete series of *Danger UXB* Special Edition

75th Commemoration Service sheet at St Paul's Cathedral, 2015

The many notes and letters written by Captain John Hannaford

John scratched off his RE badges in the photo below.

He was so angry not to have received recognition for his dangerous work that blew up and maimed his colleagues and nearly killed him.

This is a collage of John's handwritten notes, his officer records with photos as a young soldier and as an elderly man on Bexhill promenade, along with a copy of his painting of the De La Warr Pavilion, which led the author to his story.